a Wall of Hate

(MADE IN USA)

Gill Gervais

BALBOA.PRESS

A DIVISION OF HAY HOUSE

Balboa Press books may be ordered through booksellers or by contacting:

Balboa Press
A Division of Hay House
1663 Liberty Drive
Bloomington, IN 47403
www.balboapress.com
1 (877) 407-4847

Print information available on the last page.

ISBN: 978-1-9822-4316-6 (sc)
ISBN: 978-1-9822-4317-3 (hc)
ISBN: 978-1-9822-4318-0 (e)

Library of Congress Control Number: 2020902882

Balboa Press rev. date: 05/22/2020

This book may be disruptive. Take heed upon entering.

This book is dedicated to

*all the brave young people uniting as one for the
tremendous task of making our world a better place*

You're never too old to make a difference.

Contents

Preface

We must begin to live in harmony with the laws that
govern the universe.

The whole planet, and especially Western civilization, is in
a deep state of transition, and the resulting state of current
crisis is a sure indication that the entire social structure of
the planet is on the brink of collapse, quickly becoming utter
chaos.

One may wonder what motivates an eighty-year-old citizen to
write a book about the present state of the world. First, I wrote
a book called *Earth Fights Back* a few years ago and realized
that people were still more interested in making money and
hating each other than they were in healing our planet and
bringing it back to health. Although I am still overwhelmed by
the reckless ways we treat the source of all that we own, that
which feeds us and keeps us alive, I have accepted the fact that
a book like *Earth Fights Back* will not change the world—and
neither will this one—but it may help us recognize the causes
of the present crisis and find remedies and ways to calm the
hungry two-headed dragon that is now roasting us. Greed,
hate, and domination have become the norm; this is probably
what some politicians refer to when they make mention of a
new world order.

My decision to write *A Wall of Hate* was not motivated by
the idea of monetary gains or possible other benefits such as
fame or recognition but by a sincere wish to communicate,
to those who are open to consider them, some of the esoteric
laws governing the universe that I have had the opportunity
and privilege to study and experience in the course of my
life. I do not expect *A Wall of Hate* to be widely read, but the

people who do read it may feel less discomfort as a result by understanding the nature of the wall and the problem of adopting an attitude of nonparticipation, which reinforces it and in some way, and assist in repairing the damage caused by this negative and dangerous phase that humanity is going through. With knowledge, people will start thinking in a way that will have positive effects on the planet and its inhabitants and will certainly improve people's personal health, happiness, and prosperity.

Since World War II, the governments of what were then the dominant countries in the world have been developing techniques introduced by scientists that came from war criminals of the Third Reich. These Nazi criminals were recruited or kidnapped by the Soviet Union and the United States for the purpose of using the knowledge and experience of the former in order to develop the military strength of the latter. Some of those recruited were former commanders of Adolf Hitler's Nazi war machine who were involved in atrocious human experiments and most certainly practiced the art of positive mind control and forced obedience. In the United States, although the process was started in the 1930s, they have crafted their esoteric knowledge into a sinister science that has been integrated into politics and big business, definitely designed to serve a small number of wealthy individuals and giant corporations.

Almost everywhere, we are now electing politicians and allowing dictators with no detectable moral standards to serve in key positions where they can shape society as they wish to serve their own purposes. In the new politics or methods of governing, truth is no longer a requirement. With the support and partnership of the hungry and controlling business called religion, politicians these days make the most aggressive criminals look like saints, even convincing the people that they are directly appointed by their God to execute a decree ordered by him, using ancient biblical texts interpreted in such a way as to appear to support their beliefs and agendas.

There is now a strong possibility that in a future not so distant, complete control of information and mass manipulation will be 100 percent legal, any form of previously free speech will be met with strict control, and severe penalties will be imposed on those perceived as opposing the regime. We are familiar with the process and the results in countries that choose to eliminate freedom of speech. It is known as a purge, where anyone not in total agreement or who criticizes the established power and laws implemented by unopposed dictatorships can be disposed of without trial or hearing.

We now have serious problems in that most people seem to have some kind of affliction that behaves like a virus, causing them to unknowingly behave in cranky, aggressive ways, repeating the programmed agendas and lies of the controlling authorities regarding immigration, racism, sexual orientation, abortion, and other issues without being conscious of what they are doing to themselves and society in the process. They are supporting either the Left or the Right, which are only two heads of the same dragon.

People have become divided by well-orchestrated political strategies and have become so inflexible in their adopted ways as to be unable to consider any other point of view or anything different or to think or act in a manner that will benefit them, instead of benefiting those at the top who are controlling them. In other words, we are so busy hating each other that we cannot perceive or combat the harm that is being done to us by a ruling minority concentrated solely on making insane profits and gaining a great number of benefits.

The universe functions according to the law of duality, and therefore we have to accept that there are two totally opposed forces at work in the created world: positive versus negative, black versus white, good versus evil, life versus death, yin versus yang, and so on. We should realize that if we are to function normally as human beings, we must accept the fact that there is a certain amount of darkness we will have to deal with if we are to develop. What is cause for concern is the present total imbalance between these forces with the negative overtaking the positive. And with the assistance of our modern communication system, the imbalance is spreading like wildfire in the Amazon rain forest. We are now electing governments that are totally in accord and dedicated to this one dream, namely, the total submission and forced obedience of the masses to central authority.

The wall of hate we are now experiencing is above all, an all-out battle between those who want to save the planet and those who want to make an immediate profit. Given the level of evolution we have reached, it is much easier to appeal to the lower instincts of people than to inspire them with fair and creative principles.

A *Wall of Hate* is not entertainment. This book may be disruptive. Take heed upon what you enter!

Introduction

Some events we experience in life are so graphic and so vivid that they refuse to remain in the past and, for a long time, are a part of daily life, affecting the way we live, our health, and our social and economic life, perhaps for the rest of our lives. There seems to be no way of escaping the graphic images that follow you, that influence your behavior your attitude and cause you to retreat into your infamous cave.

In my late thirties, I experienced such a life-transforming event with the death of my best friend and business partner in an aircraft accident, which led to a complete collapse of the business we were operating. Being the junior partner, I was unable to operate the flight school by myself, which eventually led me to severe financial difficulties. Seeing the graphic image of my friend with his forehead almost completely gone and with his brain showing was an experience that is still with me after many years, although it no longer has the paralyzing effect it had on me at that time.

I experienced firsthand what it is like to be an outcast. I also experienced something I would not wish upon anyone else: not being able to provide adequately for my family. Suzanne, my life partner of fifty years, stayed with me for the whole journey. After moving to a strange town without much money left and three children to support, we walked into a rented apartment that did not have a piece of furniture in it. We only had funds to purchase the most urgently needed items. I soon got a job as a logging machine operator and was given an advance in pay, which permitted us to resume a normal life. The switch in jobs from a commercial pilot / flight instructor to a logger was quite a shock but getting tired from the harsh and demanding work in the bush kept me from constantly reliving the past. It also stabilized our financial situation to some degree.

I was a member of several groups and fraternities that claim to be dedicated to mutual help and support, but being a financial failure classified me as an outcast. The rejection was palpable. I am, however, thankful to one fraternity for the great lesson they taught me. This was the period when I learned to take responsibility for my actions, call my own shots, and rely on nobody else except myself and, of course, my wife.

At that time, working as a logger, I fully realized what damage and devastation was being done to our public forests, and I started thinking about doing something to help the forests recover from the devastation caused by deforestation. Eventually, Suzanne and I started a business in the alternative energy sector, selling and installing wind generators and solar panels. I was still working in forestry as I had to subsidize the store in order to stay afloat, but overall it was an enjoyable experience that lasted until oil companies started to take over the solar panels market, buying companies that were building them. Almost overnight, the cost of solar panels went up to the point where we could not sell any at the new price, we had to ask for them. Soon our supplier was forced to go out of business. I vowed at that time that my family would always come first but that I would work toward the recovery of the planet's ecosystem to the best of my abilities.

I listened to what scientists had to say about global warming, avoiding coming to any definite conclusions and or an acceptance of unproven facts. I have read countless books dealing with pollution of our planet, I have worked at and supervised reforestation operations, and I am part of an association that is not labeled as an environment protection agency but that instills in its members a deep respect for our planet and all life-forms living on it. All this gradually turned me into a worker dedicated to improving our ecosystem and the social aspect of our civilization.

It is now widely accepted that the population explosion, the technical revolution, and the total willingness to ignore the future consequences of our actions has put the ecosystem of our planet on a collision course with our modern world. The collision has already occurred, and we are starting to harvest the results of our past negligence and inaction in the face of obvious warnings. Climate change is real, although it is not recognized as such by conservative governments. We are now electing leaders who have no regard for the fragile ecosystem of Earth and are tolerating self-appointed dictators, even supporting them in their destructive work. For example, who or what could stop Brazil from destroying the lungs of the planet known as the Amazon rain forests? This massive deforestation taking place in the rain forests also involves the genocide of the traditional tribes still living there.

The global catastrophic environmental events now taking place are almost at emergency level and are more dangerous than anything we have ever faced before, even the deadliest wars we've fought, and have the potential to annihilate all forms of life on earth for a long time. Since the carbon dioxide (CO_2) we have been emitting for so long exceeds the capacity of the remaining forests to absorb, it has been absorbed by our oceans and lakes, with the result that the oceans are now saturated with carbon and polluted with oil-derived products and plastics, which are killing many forms of life. Fishes are desperately trying to adapt by moving to cooler waters. The waters of the Great Lakes are also quickly becoming toxic as poison algae are now everywhere near the shores and on the beaches.

In studying the impact humankind can have on nature, we should also consider nature itself and the cyclic occurrences to which the earth is submitted, which could also be a factor as important as our actions are. In a former book, *Earth Fights Back*, I detailed some of these cycles and their effects on the earth. This, however, could be considered pure speculation, because now science agrees with the presence of these cycles but has not conducted any research into the effects they have on the increase in temperature on the planet. We only should stick with what we think we know for sure if our wish is to avoid having to deal with the consequences of our past actions. The wall of hate we have built is making us blind enough to the transformation of our planet into a highly toxic environment.

Recently I experienced another life-changing event, surviving a medical condition that I was not expected to survive. During the long wait for surgery and the subsequent long recovery period, both filled with incredible pain, I kept visualizing my life as I wanted it to become without asking questions about how this was to happen. I refrained from becoming depressed, and despite the attachments I had to wear and the pain, I remained active and in relatively good physical condition. The result was that I fully recovered and, at age eighty, I now enjoy near-perfect health. Sometimes I am judged to be a much younger person, accomplishing tasks and tackling work usually associated with people half my age. Credit for my survival must be given to our modern advanced medical system, which I successfully reconciled with the vast knowledge of medicine held by the ancients. I now consider myself as being on an extension and decided to live whatever days are granted to me in the pursuit of happiness for others and the health of our Mother Earth.

It may be getting late. The world did not listen to Cousteau, nor did they listen to Al Gore or all the others who gave warnings. Why would they listen to me? We should continue working with the possibility of a planetary recovery in the hope that our personal actions will soften the blows when they come.

With these new movements involving giant parades, strikes, and protests, it is evident that the generation now coming of age is ready for action and willing to work toward changing things. This is good as older generations seem incapable of thinking differently to place limits on the incredible power corporations currently have over governments. We, the older ones, are still too interested in making money and amassing a fortune, and therefore we go along with the long-standing status quo. One problem, however, is that this new generation so eager for change seriously lacks direction. They will probably block roads and confront authorities who will not surrender without a fight, thereby generating violent reactions. They need to present a workable, plausible plan on how they are going to change our planet for the better.

There are, of course, many organizations working toward change that are presenting our youths with plans to exert pressure on governments, mostly by submitting petitions, organizing parades, and holding news conferences where it is openly stated that the people will no longer tolerate the devastation of the planet. Although this must be done to a certain extent, these are not the kind of actions that will make much of a difference in the long run, except to raise us up one against the other and place us in a state of violence and retaliation. Unfortunately, deep changes will not be made until we are forced by the results of climate change or of global war to transform ourselves into new beings willing to work together toward a better society. In other words, survival may be the deciding factor that will force us to change our world. More on this later when we consider likely scenarios of nuclear war and the likely results.

*   *   *

The year was 1945. The Allies had defeated the evilest empire in the history of humankind. Everyone was ecstatic, positive, enthusiastic, and looking ahead to a bright future. To most people, everything was deemed possible. Everyone was looking forward to creating and living in a society administered by morally responsible individuals where everyone would have a chance at fame and fortune or, short of that, enjoy a good level of happiness, health, and prosperity. In the United States, they called it the American dream.

Yes, the good times were here, and everyone thought that they would stay with us permanently as we possessed the right formula to create the environment and the way of life we desired.

Our military personnel returned home joyful amid the popular feeling that we lived in a country where the horrors committed by our former enemies could never happen. The abundance of food and supplies, along with almost free gasoline, greatly improved methods of transportation and communication, created what is now known as the baby boom. Everyone wanted to raise a family with lots of children who would carry on the virtuous traditions and be capable of defeating any monster empire that would dare rear its ugly head again. Yes, the folks were happy!

And good times they were. Almost everyone had an automobile, money was plentiful, and one did not have to go without a job as there were so many good ones to get if one was not satisfied with one's present employment.

Then came rock and roll with Elvis Presley, the Beatles, the Rolling Stones, Bob Dylan, and many others, and everyone was happily dancing to the new and very entertaining songs and productions. The drive-in theater, which was quite an innovation, provided affordable, pleasant entertainment. Housing was expanding, and we had comfortable homes to go to, along with a shorter workweek with ample time for vacation and good times with family or friends. People of that generation can still remember the excitement of the first brand-new shiny Mustang or concerts like Woodstock where they experienced total freedom and exerted their right to party and be a little wild without fear of religious or government intervention or control. They developed a concept of superiority and that is still with us today but is now expressed more as nationalism, patriotism and partisanship.

The baby boomers even created an institution that would prevent war from happening again. Despite the many criticisms directed against the United Nations, the UN has been successful in exerting some kind of influence over the affairs of the world at large and has contributed in avoiding several conflicts that could have become serious enough to resort to military confrontation between formerly allied countries. Other countries where any form of slavery existed, approved by dictatorship or arising from internal conflicts, were provided help in the form of funding, expert advice, and military action if it was judged necessary. Of course, there were conflicts and wars, most of which could have been avoided, but overall the West was free, strong, and safe, and the future looked even brighter with the certainty that we could never be attacked on our homeland and would never have to experience a holocaust like Europe had.

But the baby boomers, being better educated than their forebears and well-fed, having total freedom to do or create anything they liked, in spite of all the benefits they were reaping from former generations who had fought for their freedom, started to develop a kind of antiestablishment attitude and became easy targets for anyone wishing to impose new and advanced concepts. The boomers were eager to accept a form of brainwashing where they perceived a more enjoyable future with almost unlimited access to produced goods.

Instead of being considered a necessary tool for any society to operate efficiently, money became an end-in-itself. People started to view it as the ultimate power, the acquisition of which would make one strong, independent, and masterful. Production of consumer goods went through the roof. Keeping up with the Joneses was an idea that became a sort of disease that affected one's happiness, self-worth, and peace of mind. One could not allow neighbors, friends, or family to own more goods or have more money. Yes, we became hooked on money, but in the process, we forgot morality, decency, fairness, and truth. Money was to be acquired by any means, even by methods that were detrimental to society in general and to certain targeted groups, and we demanded more and more of it—and this without much regard for the environment or the consequences of our actions, as ecology was not considered a priority or even something worth considering in the first place as Mother Earth would provide and would surely replace the resources we had used. We were making big bucks, and without our knowledge, we were just following a clever pattern designed to turn us into money and consumer goods addicts. And it worked. Corporations were making record profits; governments could direct people into dreaming of a better system, especially before an election; and we became more and more centered on *me* and gradually showed less and less concern for organized society. The quality of our infrastructures, or social issues was considered as being the responsibility of elected officials, who were still perceived as being strong and honest.

We are now living in a society where almost all has become political and the ensuing profound division has cranked us up one against another. It is difficult to have a conversation with anyone without its turning to politics, racism, and other subjects so dear to the brainwashed who often express their beliefs in strong, bully-like ways using words that hardly disguises a threat and suggests that the other person should adopt their point of view. These people usually support leaders who are rich, powerful, mouthy, totally ignorant of social environmental or moral issues, and devoid of anything that resembles fairness to the people who elected them.

Yes, in 1945, the United States brought most of its military and equipment back home with a horizon of lasting peace, but it also brought back something much more sinister.

The end of the war was followed by a period of great prosperity with abundant goods and food. This period was also marked with new technology that completely changed the way food was produced. Farming with the help of chemicals became the norm and helped produce large amounts of food—almost perfect crops—with minimum loss. Raising animals for human consumption by using growth hormones and antibiotics turned farming into a profitable business with high returns on investment. What we did not consider at that time is that abundance of food for any species translates into offspring and proliferation to the point where they destroy their environment and their source of food. This is common to all species, including ours. But I am getting way ahead of myself here.

Operation Paperclip

T he writing was on the wall. After Adolf Hitler's failure to invade Russia, with the disastrous result of the Battle of Stalingrad for the Germans and the entrance of the United States into the war, military and technical advantages began to shift in favor of the Allies, now greatly reinforced. After the Allied invasion in Normandy on D-Day, it became apparent to German leaders and Nazi commanders, except for Hitler, that the war was lost and that it was just a matter of time before they would have to surrender.

A few of Hitler's generals and advisers approached him, trying to present him with obvious facts, and suggested that he should seriously consider a negotiated settlement to end the conflict. Such a settlement could have had the effect of reducing or easing the severe sanctions that would certainly be imposed, especially during the transition period from war to peace. They suggested the submission of a treaty that would guarantee lasting peace in Europe and even offer the Allies some form of collaboration in rebuilding the countries devastated by the war. Hitler flatly refused to accept their advice. Those making these suggestions soon realized that further display of this kind of weakness would make them prime candidates for a purge.

There is no point in discussing further whatever actions took place before the end of the war as these are abundantly documented. However, it is well-known that the Soviets invaded Germany ahead of the other Allies. German scientists, engineers, specialized workers, and researchers willingly surrendered to them, offering their specialized services in exchange for their lives. Most of these scientists were war criminals who would probably be facing military trials with

1

possible execution if captured. The Soviets realized that those men of knowledge could provide them with a marked advantage in the development of weapons technology as some were spies, researchers in the field of mind control, doctors, rocket scientists, and specialists in weaponry. They were well trained, fresh from having fought what was probably the deadliest war in history.

The Soviets, not content to accept the services of those who surrendered, started to kidnap them, offering them and their families, safety and relative freedom. They also developed a recruiting project they called Operation Osoaviakhim. In some of their operations, whole families were kidnapped, imprisoned, and held as hostages, leaving the head of these families no other choice than to work for the Soviets under their stated conditions. The Soviets "recruited" twenty-two hundred people, gave them citizenship, and protected many of them from being detected and brought to trial at Nuremberg.

The Americans soon realized that the Soviet Union, through their aggressiveness in acquiring war materials and recruiting scientists, researchers, and specialized workers from Germany, would soon be the dominant force on the planet if not opposed by the United States and its allies. If this path to dominance were permitted to continue unchecked, it would put the Soviets in a position to occupy and annex a good portion, if not all, of Europe and to become a serious threat to the Western world, even across the Atlantic.

The First Response: Project Overcast

As World War II was entering its final stages, US and British forces teamed up to scour Germany for military, technical, and scientific development and people who could be helpful in the development of their respective military forces. As the Allies progressed with the occupation of Germany, they were followed by a group called the Combined Intelligence Objectives Subcommittee (CIOS), who were confiscating documents, war

2

materials, and any chemical weapons or weapons of mass destruction they could find. They seized and confiscated research facilities that had been unlocked and made available by the Allied forces. By sheer luck, a document was recovered from a toilet in Bonn that was an almost complete list or catalogue of engineers, scientists, and researchers whose work had been assigned to the Third Reich.

Thanks to now declassified documents, it is possible to be informed about what really took place—the reasons these projects were created and allowed. It is not within the framework of *A Wall of Hate* to judge the value of these projects, as it is most probable that inaction would mean the Soviets would probably win the Cold War as they were already in possession of German intelligence and technologies for the development of better conventional weapons and long-range rockets, more effective tanks, aircraft and ships.

The Soviets were also interested in mind control, which was not invented by the Nazis but was researched and perfected by individuals, including Hitler, who had contacts and had studied psychological methods of mind control. These efforts included so-called esoteric organizations that at the time were considered secret societies and that are now blamed for our present crisis. Unfortunately, these mind control techniques, so efficient in brainwashing and used widely by the Third Reich, were also imported to the United States under the cover of Operation Overcast, renamed Operation Paperclip and implemented within the CIA under that name, later to be renamed Operation MKUltra. This operation was dedicated to the formation of superspies using the techniques based on those the Nazis had developed from their experiments in concentration camps.

In the United States, Operation Overcast was created in July 1945 by the Joint Chiefs of Staff. Even though they were not authorized or sanctioned to do so, they started to recruit German scientists, engineers, and research technicians who were able to contribute considerable intellectual resources, especially in medicine, warfare, space programs, and intelligence, and relocated them to the United States.

President Truman later approved and sanctioned the operation. The president's approval was subject to a condition that no member or former member of the Nazi Party would be granted asylum. But after being dispatched to the CIA, the army, research centers, and weapons manufacturing corporations, their records were whitewashed or erased, and these refugees were given freedom and put on the government payroll with identity protection and family security. Some sixteen hundred people were relocated to the United States and Canada, given jobs, and protected from scrutiny. Former spies of the Third Reich worked with or for the CIC, later called the CIA. Some were even returned to their country of origin with a US or Canadian passport and a new identity, where they continued to work for their new hosts and protectors.

President Truman commented in 1963 that he never regretted approving the project, and if called upon again to make such a decision, his choice would remain unchanged. It is obvious that former Nazi war criminals had entered the United States without the consent or knowledge of the population, and in many cases, civil American scientists and technicians were laid off in order to make room for the newcomers. It could be argued that without their help, the Cold War would have been lost and the US space program could not have developed the technology that enabled NASA to put a person on the moon. One fact, however, stands out: none of these newcomers has been prosecuted or questioned about their Nazi involvement.

One of these men was Arthur Rudolph, who was the officer responsible for the rocket team that developed the V-2 for the Nazis and who had had access to slave labor in concentration camps. He and his team, after willingly surrendering to the United States, developed the V-5 missile and were instrumental in the success of the US space-race program. Rudolph was the dominant figure in the development of rockets that would eventually permit humankind to walk on the moon. He was highly decorated in the United States and almost got the most meritorious medal awarded to Americans, until his former involvement with the Nazis became known.

Another addition was Dr. Josef Mengele, also known as the Angel of Death, who liberally used torture on war prisoners in concentration camps and developed techniques that in a few hours could cause any individual to dissociate into multiple personalities, respond to posthypnotic suggestions or commands, and execute the proposed actions. Many others could be mentioned, but that would only be repeating information on these projects that is freely available on the internet is, for the most part, reliable.

The Aim of Operation Paperclip

Operation Paperclip is the code name that the United States used during the final stage of the war and afterward to designate the search conducted by intelligence and the military in Germany to find scientists, engineers, technicians, and psychologists to be recruited and brought to the United States. The Joint Intelligence Objectives Agency immediately put these people to work. They were placed on the US payroll without the public's knowledge.

No detailed account of the process will be rendered here, as there are many good books available dealing exclusively with this operation, but a few questions should be answered to clarify or even justify the US government's actions.

Did the United States Really Have a Choice?

The answer to this is debatable. It was considered then that the developers of advanced weapons that nearly had given a victory to the Third Reich were needed in the United States.

The Soviets were also engaged in the same recruiting process, and it was just a matter of time before they achieved world supremacy unless they were to face serious opposition from the United States. The alternative must have been seriously considered before giving war criminals a free pass, a job on the US payroll, protection for their families, and relative freedom to create or continue projects started or implemented in Germany. Their knowledge and expertise did in fact give the United States a boost in the development of biological, chemical, and atomic weapons and helped the United States make a huge leap forward in the development of communications, satellites, medicine, and—unfortunately for us now—mind control.

Why Was It Kept Secret?

This project had to be kept secret because of the outrage it would have created if made public. The secrecy also gave these imported scientists and technicians the privilege of working undercover in the United states without being harassed by some of the veterans and other patriotic groups. Time has passed, and those who would have been against the project are no longer with us. But without their contributions, the United States could not have developed the sophisticated military arsenal that has made the US presidents the most powerful persons in the world.

Please note that I have not studied the declassified documents to a great extent as the time required would prevent me from writing about it. I have read enough under the Freedom of Information Act to be almost certain that what has been made public did really happen and that actions taken then are really part of our history, even if some of the articles published on the internet sound like conspiracy theories. Some surely are misleading, but most of the information published on various websites can be reasonably believed to be true. *A Wall of Hate* is not about the recruiting operations that took place between 1945 and 1964 but about the influence it had on the development of present-day divisive politics, effectively used by Hitler and refined to a science by the Americans. New right-wing governments' political policies based on global and individual brainwashing could be the final onslaught of our planet's ecosystem and the last nail in the coffin for the concepts of democracy, freedom, and equitable society.

The Nazis' Profound Knowledge of Mind Control

Germany had a long history of interest and involvement in esoteric organizations, but in the early twentieth century, some of these researchers who had been longtime members of one among many secret societies and who were probably in possession of knowledge related to mind control began to intensify their research into psychology and psychiatry with an eye toward the application to warfare, even to the extent of exploring occult practices to achieve control of the masses. This inevitably led the researchers to the ancient knowledge expressed in Kabbalah, magic, alchemy, and hypnotism and the methods used by then hidden organizations to experiment on modifications in a subject's personality and the possibility of mass control.

Adolf Hitler was one of these researchers. He had the ability to speak forcefully and convincingly, even to the point of presenting a complete program of lies and deceit that would eventually modify the global thinking of the population to form a group of fanatically brainwashed people who were ready to accept and support him in everything he wanted or stated. He called this process National Socialism, which was much more than a political party. In the process of building his team, he recruited Nazis-turned-occultists such as Baron Rudolf Freiherr von Sebottendorf, Jorg Lane Bienbenfels, Guido von List, Dietrich Eckart, and Karl Hausherer, all of whom had immersed themselves in the philosophies of the Theosophical Society. This, in fact, developed into a research team that would conduct incredibly cruel experiments on prisoners of war and anyone else who was considered different or undesirable to the mother cause.

The goal here is not to go through the history of the Third Reich or discuss how their methods moved to the United States and the Western world, but to demonstrate the effects these actions have had on our present society and on the world at large, and how the wall of hate was created in Germany long before it came to the United States.

Where Did the Knowledge of Mind Control Come from in the First Place?

The laws used in mind control are ingrained in the basic laws of the universe. The soul that enters the body when the infant inhales his first breath is part of the universal soul, which is the same in every human—and in this sense only are people created equal. The soul is cosmic in nature and is meant to assist and guide a person in the journey through the learning process. Each personality undertakes this journey in his or her temporary residence, the body, where we all must work with the principles of matter in order to learn the deeper laws and evolve accordingly through trials and lessons.

The subconscious will create anything, act on anything, and bring into the person's life whatever the conscious mind has accepted as true. The law sounds so simple as to be easily discarded as fantasy or one of the things we are unable to understand or play with. The reverse is also true; whatever the subconscious mind has accepted through suggestions while the psychic self was in an altered state of consciousness will determine one's beliefs and actions. There is a level of consciousness within every human that automatically causes the blood to flow, causes the heart to beat, and regulates all bodily functions. The body is preprogrammed to perform these functions without conscious direction. Our state of health and happiness depends a lot on the cooperation of the conscious mind (brain) with the master within in order to maintain a reasonable state of health, peace, happiness, and prosperity, but the master within can also be programmed from within and from without by clever manipulation. The initiatory process of some of the so-called secret societies can accomplish this. It can transform the outer and inner personality and beliefs of a willing candidate.

Later we will go deeper into the workings of these laws and see how the principles of programming or reprogramming the subconscious mind can be used for good or for bad without discrimination and how they have been used in the past for evil purposes. The statement to be retained at this time is that your subconscious can be programmed or brainwashed by you or by someone else. It takes courage and determination to regain freedom after having been brainwashed by outside persuasions because you perceive these as being of your own creation and they have all the characteristics of an ingrained habit that could be difficult to overcome. Later, we will see how mass control functions and how one can become conscious of it and take action to eventually change into a freethinker, which will allow one to understand the reasons we are serving or repeating the agendas and programs that will, whether in the short or long run, only benefit some kind of central authority that controls our thinking and actions in order to thrive.

The Methods Tested and Developed in Project Bluebird with the Collaboration of the Nazis

Project Bluebird was approved and put in place shortly after the end of the war by the director of the CIA for the purpose of developing more efficient methods, better weapons, and the ability of mass control, all of which were used by Nazis during the war.

It is a well-known fact that during the late nineteenth and early twentieth centuries, Germans became interested and were quite active in ancient organizations and their teachings, which sometimes dated back many centuries. Many of them became celebrities, either as writers, philosophers, artists, heads of powerful companies, or politicians, or in some other exalted position. What people did not realize at that time is that the secrets so well kept by those so-called secret societies to prevent them from being used for doubtful purposes could be applied either for good or for bad. The laws of the subconscious are totally neutral and, once mastered, give the operator a power to be used as he or she decides.

A memo published by the CIA but kept secret until it became declassified details some of the questions that were asked and explored with the assistance or under the direction of Germans, such as the following:

1. Can we, in a matter of hours or days, induce a programmed suggestion to make a subject perform actions for our benefit?
2. Can we, by way of posthypnotic suggestion, have a subject perform acts or make statements that are contrary to his own moral code?
3. Could we seize a subject and, in the space of hours, make him perform acts like hijacking an airplane, bombing a ship or a subway, or performing a mass shooting?
4. Can we induce total amnesia?
5. Can we alter a person's personality?
6. How can we induce fear to make a subject totally agree to any command given?
7. Can we change someone's personality and have the subject gather information on our behalf and even bring back valuable documents?
8. Can we use drugs to place a subject in a state of receptivity, where he will readily accept the changes we suggest?
9. Can we make a subject lose his power of reasoning and freedom of mind without his being aware of it by using psychological, emotional, and intellectual manipulation while he is in altered states of consciousness?

10. Can controlled repetition change perception of facts?
11. Can controlled repetition alter behavior?

Other methods were probably on the CIA's agenda. The effects of torture and deprivation were probably studied. Unbelievably, torture and deprivation were made legal in the United States during the George W. Bush era to be used in enhanced interrogations.

National Socialism

> Anyone who interprets National Socialism merely as a political movement almost knows nothing about it. It is more than a religion. It is a determination to create a new man.
>
> —Adolf Hitler

From 1933 to 1945, Nazi Germany's government led by Adolf Hitler planned and put into practice a longtime dream of enforced nationalism that combined territorial expansion and claims of racial superiority of the Aryan race. This led to a program that would eliminate those considered undesirable. Although other groups were targeted, Jews were considered the greatest threat to the purity of the Aryan race. The effectiveness of this program is well-known. It is now believed that six million Jews were eliminated.

Mass Sterilization Program

In order to preserve the purity of the race, a mass sterilization program was implemented to ensure that those considered genetically impure would be sterilized to prevent them from producing offspring that would contaminate the race and be a burden to the ruling body and the war effort.

Individuals afflicted by what was considered birth or hereditary defects were found and effectively neutralized.

Those suffering from feeblemindedness, dementia, manic-depressive disorder, physical deformity, chronic alcoholism, or homosexuality, including a great number of citizens who were suspected of behaving in an antisocial manner, had to submit to sterilization surgery. An estimated four hundred thousand Germans are thought to have been processed between 1939 and 1945 under what the Nazis called the racial hygiene operation.

The preceding statements are not intended to revive the horrors of the last world war or to blame the German people for what has taken place as they were in fact brainwashed as Americans are now. Instead the intent is to show the striking similarities between the effective mass control tools used by the Nazis and the ones that are used in the Western world today, especially within the United States.

The Nazi Wall of Hate

As can easily be seen, the rulers of the Third Reich created an impenetrable wall of hate so powerful and so well organized in its operation that it took the rest of the world several years to tame its devastating power and reestablish some kind of order out of the chaos it had created, both on the European continent and across the rest of the world.

One thing that needs to be said about this wall of hate is that Germany had created before and during the war. Hitler did not have to deal with much opposition from within as the whole country was seemingly agreeable to his programs. Extreme National Socialism was widely accepted by the population, who believed it was beneficial to them. In other words, Hitler had unified the country and then turned it into a formidable war machine. Remember that the war didn't start with gas chambers, concentration camps, and invasion of other countries. It started with a clever politician dividing the people one against another. It started with intolerance, racism, hate speeches, and aggressiveness.

Any US president now faces a different situation as the turmoil generated from such divisive techniques is draining the life out of white supremacy and gun-ownership-oriented nationalism. The United States is now facing a situation that could very well lead to civil war and the ultimate breakup of the country. Since its foundation, the United States of America has been recognized as the world's bastion of freedom, tolerance, and friendship. This may be the reason why its citizens react to the installation of a dictatorship in a different way than other countries would. It will be extremely difficult for any president to unify the country with principles of totalitarianism, even with the contribution of religious groups and large corporations, in a land that has been a bastion of democracy for centuries. Building walls of greed and hate, along with international borders and intimidation, may generate tremendous energy temporarily, but the inevitable result will be the victory of one or the other opposing force. Hitler, on the other hand, did not have to deal with division as the whole country was unified in their belief that the Aryan race was superior and that what they claimed was just and even decreed by superior and unseen forces. The United States of America and the rest of Western civilization has become too racially diversified to be united unless they develop a new racial tolerance. A war with a common enemy could unify the country even with all its racial differences, but this tactic has been used too many times.

The Original Sources of the Mind Control Arts

This may sound weird to some, but the original source of mind control or mind programming is ancient traditional esoteric groups or organizations that are now blamed and accused of secretly ruling the planet by putting into practice unseen, unexplained, mysterious knowledge acquired from doubtful inexplicable powers. Here we see the application of one of the most prominent and powerful tools, that of accusing other people or other groups of practicing the unethical methods of subtle control that one is effectively using.

Gill Gervais

The Thule Society

It is at best difficult to trace the origin of this mysterious group, or to search its history, or even to make sense of the teachings of this order. The Thule Society was founded in 1919 under the direction and leadership of a German occultist named Dietrich Eckart, who was himself a member of many other esoteric societies such as the Freemasons, the Rosicrucians, the Illuminati, and the alchemists. Adolf Hitler joined the order in 1919 and was appointed as the leader of the New World Order. This theme of the New World Order is still present today within a mysterious group called the Skull and Bones society or fraternity.

Much could be said about the history and background of the society, but to elaborate would serve no useful purpose here. There is ample documentation on the internet about the Thule Society. Whatever may be added here would be secondhand, unverified information. And in any event, it is difficult to differentiate truth from speculation or propaganda.

What is in my estimation the closest to the truth is what history has given us. The Thule Society's core beliefs seem to be compatible with the writings of Madame Blavatsky, who wrote that she was in communication with a hierarchy of supermen who had survived the destruction of Atlantis and were the secret chiefs of an order that would soon regain their rightful place in the world. These masters were gifted with some sort of advanced spirituality with their superpowers and higher levels of consciousness intact. According to Blavatsky, these supermen were the survivors of an ancient race called the Aryans. The Thule Society, through Adolf Hitler and other Nazi leaders, claimed that the present German nation descended directly from this ancient and superior race. The notion that the Aryans were a superior race that should reclaim their place as leaders of the world was readily accepted by the German population. This gave the Nazis the incredible advantage of achieving national unity without fights, resistance, or opposition as the citizens saw themselves as a master race.

Although national unity is an asset that will help when leading a country into war, conditioning of the population and the designation of a common enemy is necessary. In almost every other war, the conditioning came from an unexpected violent attack from another country or group that would force the victim country to retaliate, but in the case of Germany just before World War II, the conditioning was achieved by way of well-orchestrated brainwashing propaganda. A monstrous wall of hate was built against the Jews, who were perceived as a common threat to be eliminated, without the need of a previous violent physical attack. At this point, the world changed dramatically, and every law created by the Nazi administration was based on fear, control, and nationalism. Hitler was regarded as a kind of demi-god and supreme commander whose words were readily obeyed and executed. Every group that could be considered a threat to his supremacy was outlawed and eliminated. This applied not only to Germany but also for most of Europe. Groups like the Freemasons, who remained undetected by the authorities, wore a pin with a flower called "forget-me-not" as a secret sign of mutual recognition, performed sometimes very dangerous undercover work that accelerated the allied victory, but other fraternal organizations went totally underground.

The Rosicrucians, who were the most prominent esoteric group in Europe during the Renaissance period, had previously moved their headquarters to the United States under the direction of H. Spencer Lewis in 1915 and are now located in what is called Rosicrucian Park in San Jose, California. Ancient and important documents have been moved from Tibet, Egypt, and other exotic places to San Jose in order to provide protection from intrusion and destruction—and therefore they were out of Hitler's reach.

The Illuminati

I cannot, in a short time, gather enough information to decide which order is the original, as many groups have adopted the name Illuminati. It may be that the Thule Society, with close contacts with this group, protected them from detection and may have been in some way integrated into this order. This is pure unverifiable speculation. It is claimed in certain types of literature that there is still a group so secret and protected by world leaders as to be undetectable. These powerful Illuminati are believed by some to be the secret rulers of the world.

How It All Started

The conscious and intelligent manipulation of the masses is an important element in a democratic society. Those who manipulate the unseen mechanism of society constitute an invisible government which is the true ruling power of a country.
—Edward Barneys "Propaganda" 1928

We are presently experiencing serious problems with friction between countries, friction between political parties within countries, and dangerous friction between individuals who have become so divided that they cannot accept or even consider the other side's point of view that differs from their narrow concept of what society should be or do. This has been brought about by clever political manipulation in collaboration with powerful corporations—and probably organized crime and religious extremists—so hungry for power and money that they use these techniques to acquire and keep their positions of power and domination. They divided the population in such a way that has kept people so busy despising each other that they have almost completely lost the ability to think for themselves or consider a benevolent society where those in need may receive temporary assistance from the state to help them get back to a normal life.

Let us consider the development of our society from the beginning, long before the German imports came, and how those German imports dramatically improved the system that was already in place. Given the one-sided nature of this system, it is nothing less than incredible that so many people are unable to see through the veil of lies, immoral acts, and brainwashing. We have finally built a society that is predominantly based on hate, war, strife, and doom instead of cooperation, goodwill, tolerance, and hope.

Let's Go Back to the 1920s

In 1928, Edward Barneys, a nephew of psychologist Carl G. Jung, published an obscure book entitled *Propaganda*. This was a sort of an essay on mass psychology and mass behavioral control through propaganda and manipulation of information. This book was never a best seller but became the marketing bible of the early twentieth century. It left a legacy that grew to become the infernal deliberate misinformation system that eventually created the roller-coaster ride of inequality we know today.

There may or may not be collusion at the top where meetings are held among top executives to improve the methods of brainwashing, but remember that all types of corruption have the same common denominators, namely, money and power, and are based on excessive profits. It's all about money and control, starting with governments that are controlled and work in collaboration with powerful corporations. We may claim that we know that misinformation and brainwashing is alive and well in our modern society, but we probably would be reluctant to admit that we let ourselves be influenced by twisted commercials and manipulated news broadcasts. There are, however, some signs that you have been unconsciously or consciously affected by media and that you are following a line of thinking presented with bias by these media. For example, war is a lucrative business, and those profiting from the business will use clever methods to convince you that war is a necessary evil. You are being programmed to view certain groups or races of people who look or act different from you as undesirable, as an enemy that must be eliminated from the face of the earth.

As presented in Barney's book, if concentration of population in large countries is to succeed, one must divide the masses into two distinct groups that are polarized between two seemingly opposed policies and two seemingly different lines of thinking. The two groups being programmed in our day are known as the Left and the Right, and the division acts as a powerful tool that stops the masses from thinking independently and acting efficiently. Individuals on both sides who are convinced that they are fighting for the right cause will go to extreme lengths to prove the superiority of their opinions, considering these to be the result of their own uninfluenced thinking and profound wisdom.

Some of your thinking and actions could be an indication that you are in fact acting as the unseen government directs you to act and think. If you eat fast food or junk food without questioning how it will affect your overall well-being and health and the health of the planet, then you have been hit. If you think that you can trust governments at any level with food supply, water supply, and honest administrative policies, then you have been hit. If you think our health-care system is trustworthy and that all doctors and pharmaceutical companies are working toward improving the quality of life, then you have been hit. If you accept without questioning the side effects of some of the medications and practices because they have been approved by the proper health or governments authorities, you have been hit. If you think you are part of an elite group that is superior to any other groups that are different from your own, you have been hit. If you think your country or the group you support within your country has a monopoly on all the wisdom and power and is the best in the world, then you have been hit. If you think that war is a necessary evil or that some groups should be eliminated from the face of the earth, then you have been seriously hit.

Barney's book was based on a good knowledge of psychology, and the methods he presented are sound and efficient, although I am not convinced that mass thinking in his era was controlled or directed. At that time the new invisible government just adapted methods used by religions and esoteric groups throughout the ages. The difference was the lack of social conscience; the new movement that used these methods did so to serve their own interests. This is not meant as praise or criticism of religion. Despite all the wars and destruction religions have been responsible for, we should also recognize the good works they have been involved in and the beneficial form of mass control they exerted.

The Standard Tools of Mass Brainwashing

Edward S. Herman and Noam Chomsky in their book *Manufacturing Consent*, published in 1988, give us a good outline of how media and information, which are supposed to serve as a system of communication and entertainment, should be transformed into a tool to inculcate individuals and their core values and integrate them into a larger society concentrated on wealth and control. Herman and Chomsky stated that the achievement of this aim requires systematic propaganda.

The key to truly effective brainwashing is to chip away at people's most fundamental awareness and feelings. Their thinking must be modified at the neurological level, so they eventually accept the desired input, take it for granted, and even defend their conviction that they are thinking for themselves. Instinct and intuition need to be impaired or destroyed by actively and endlessly encouraging external awareness.

Some of the techniques often used in advertising:

Speed

People should become dependent on external input for as many decisions as possible and speeding up the messages will cause disorientation in the recipient's thinking process.

Repetition

Being bombarded with hundreds of thousands of messages each day conditions a person to eventually accept the stimulus and make it his or her own reality. A message heard once can be forgotten easily. If heard a thousand times, it will attach itself to the person's brain waves and will become not only acceptable but also part of the individual's regular baggage and beliefs.

A Choice of Content

You must decide what you want people to believe and make sure that any choices you give them are within a framework that will ensure your desired result. Give them the illusion of choice. This is one of the great deceptions widely used by economic systems, politicians, entertainers, athletes, and news broadcasters.

Humor

Presenting a message with a touch of humor appeals to the lowest common denominator. Make sure that all messages contain model conflict resolution with easy solutions and avoid anything that would make the targets think about or doubt the results if they follow your advice or buy your products.

Putting the Target in a Receptive State

A couch potato is an easy target. If you keep people passive and comfortable, they will readily accept your suggestions and solutions as the magic elixir that will cure all that ails them. To override their thinking and analytical faculties, it is best to sound benevolent as though you have only their best interests at heart. There are other effective ways to put individuals or even crowds into such a receptive state and cause them to readily accept almost anything presented, whether it is true or not.

Sensory Stimulation

Use no story lines with meaning or purpose. Keep the narrative simple and easy to understand. Above all, make certain that there is no cultural, societal, or global content that would create conflict with the idea of comfort derived from consumption. Never suggest that the targets are responsible for their own actions or choices. Do not even hint that they could be involved in shaping their own future or reality or improving their station in life. You want the recipients to accept the ideas presented in your message, while giving them the illusion of having made a free choice.

Sensationalism

If it is superficial, make it look sensational, and if possible, use a lot of colors. Information bytes should be small and to the point. Most people are already programmed to receive these frequent chunks of information and have probably developed attention deficit disorder set in motion by several decades of watching television, listening to radio and other media, and otherwise being exposed to mass information and entertainment sources.

Working on the Emotions

Make the message emotional. Nothing drives people into action or inaction better than an emotional response. Avoid logic and rationality. Clips like "We the people" are proven winners. Real winners also include logos, slogans, and flashed bits of information. These act as preconditioners.

Truth

Regardless of the content of the message, whether it is the truth, a half-truth, or an outright lie, if you repeat it often enough, it will eventually be accepted as true—a favorite tactic in our day.

Using Questions that Suggest the Answer

"You don't suppose that Albert could be responsible for the missing funds, do you?" Sure enough, most people will start thinking of Albert as someone who is untrustworthy and possibly dishonest. No definite or positive statement has been made, but the desired result is palpable, especially for the intended victim.

Promote the idea that "the truth will set you free." Even if you are lying, this will program the listener or viewer to place complete trust in the message and the source. Throw around words such as *cult, marginal,* and *brainwashing,* and make sure the recipient believes that you would never descend to such low levels of behavior.

Creating a Distressing Situation

Present short distressing lines describing problems for which there are no immediate remedies or cures except to go shopping, vote for the allegedly perfect candidate, believe the preacher, buy the new car, go to the sports event, or do anything else that may be presented.

Appealing to People's Basic Instincts

This one is powerful, and commanding marketing programs are often based on this technique. Modern politics intensively appeals to our lowest instincts and rarely to the best instincts present in every one of us.

Shifting the Blame

By accusing competitors of using dubious concepts you yourself are effectively using, you shift the blame onto them. This will seriously harm their image while promoting your claims. (This tactic is widely used in politics.)

We are exposed daily to most of these mind programming tools. The sources vary but they include media, early education, parental input, educational institutions and many others like:

Media

Nearly everyone knows that we are being manipulated and brainwashed by the media and the system, but we fail to realize the profound effects this can have on mass consciousness. We are now facing a serious epidemic of depression and a rate of suicide that is nothing short of shattering, this despite all the benefits that modern technology has made available to us that are supposed to make our lives so much easier and more pleasant.

Early Brainwashing

From the earliest days of our lives, we are molded by traditions and beliefs that will constantly drive us to be competitive and adapted to society. These will stay with us for the rest of our lives unless we make a conscious decision to change them. Depression is, after all, the belief or conviction that we cannot compete effectively or adjust to accepted standards, whether financial, social, or emotional. From the earliest age, we are programmed to believe that we are worthless and not a real part of the society unless we conform to certain beliefs and practices. There is also a harmful belief programmed in us from the beginning that power does not reside within us and that we do not possess the ability to control or direct the events that will shape our own lives.

Parental Input

Parents have a great responsibility for developing the mind of a child. The first six years of life are very important as beliefs and habits acquired during this period last a lifetime and are extremely difficult to change if the person seeks to do so when he or she becomes an adult.

Educational Institutions

Students are trained to strive and compete on tests and to obtain grades that will permit them to graduate, land a good job, and make a living. There is little incentive or training to develop a student's ability to deal with real-world or business situations later in life.

The Criminal Justice System

One must conform to certain legislated standards of conduct. The criminal justice system has now become big business. Failure to conform can have severe consequences to one's freedom, even for minor offenses such as the use or possession of certain plants that have been declared illegal.

Government

While governments are necessary to administer countries and act in the best interests of the majority, relying on government teaches us to shift our own responsibilities onto elected officials and ask them to make decisions for us, which creates a certain form of dependency on external forces. As almost everyone is now aware, governments do what is good for governments and not what is good for the people.

Religion

Despite some of the positive work done by religion, it teaches us to rely or depend on forces totally outside ourselves and to trust in something that we don't fully understand, while some of the religious leaders use clever manipulations of ancient texts and superstition to convince us that they are the gifted ones with a direct line to the unseen powers above. They program people into believing that by following them and making material contributions, they may have access to a permanent state of pure ecstasy in the hereafter.

War

The assumed necessity of war simply convinces us that the world is full of violence and that the only way one can function is by mimicking this violence in everyday life.

Financial Institutions

Our modern financial institutions are designed to exert control over the masses and are being run by a very greedy group of individuals. Failure to conform to their standards is probably one of the main causes of depression and suicide.

As Henry Ford said, *"It is well enough that people of the nation do not understand our banking and monetary system, for if they did, I believe there would be a revolution before tomorrow morning."*

Large Crowds/Gatherings

One of the most potent tools in marketing or behavior modification are gatherings of large crowds where subjects can easily be induced into a mild to medium state of subconsciousness or an open, receptive state where they can be programmed to accept the orator's views without argument. One of the preferred methods is to have designated supporters start chanting slogans, such as "USA, USA," and repeating it until the crowd picks it up and starts chanting. It often starts with a mild form of a slogan that appeals to questionable type of nationalism and is soon upgraded to the more malicious type that directly appeals to hate, the lowest instinct in humans. The slogans are varied and could be something such as, "Lock him up. Lock him up." Some can be vicious tools meant to destroy an opponent's reputation or credibility and cause him or her irreparable damage.

The Two-Minute Hate

In his book *1984*, George Orwell describes an event that was presented daily to the masses by Big Brother. It was called "the two-minute hate." It was presented at different times and was compulsory to watch and listen to. The "hate" was projected on screens or to crowds at large gatherings. Nothing positive or any kind of program was presented. It simply showed the face of Big Brother's perceived enemy, to either ridicule him or portray him as extremely evil. The main character, Winston, could not avoid these two-minute hates because they were compulsory. They turned him into a jumping, grimacing, violent lunatic ready and willing to kill anyone.

In our modern society, we have the equivalent of these two-minute hate sessions in the form of political brainwashing hate messages, especially during an election campaign, most of the time paid for by the very people the candidates are trying to brainwash. Yes, the messages are messages of hate and they are meant to destroy the reputation and credibility of an opponent, regardless of truth, decency, or morality. With the help of our miraculous communication system, they are spreading like the plague. It is not a very ethical method, but it is effective. We now even have the ten-second hate in the form of tweets that can destroy an opponent, control the ups and downs of the stock market, the price of precious metals, the value of currencies, and influence the delicate balance between countries. Tweeting is a powerful tool that has the potential of generating insane profits for those who have advance knowledge of the resulting chaos. It can create a form of manipulation to the value of financial commodities. It could even start a war.

To show how this hate wave is spreading, Canada, which has always been known for moderation in everything, totally abandoned this principle during the last federal election campaign. Prime Minister Justin Trudeau wore a bulletproof vest following death threats. The minister of the environment also received threats and faced such harassment from supporters of a carbon-oriented economy as to make her life extremely difficult. In my own riding, the woman who ran for Member of Parliament was constantly attacked verbally and was threatened a few times. Here are her own words:

> During the campaign, my day was never complete until I was cussed at two or three times. I had two men tell me they wished Justin Trudeau would get shot in the head. My seventeen-year-old son and his girlfriend had a guy in Elliot Lake tell them to get off his step. My older son had someone tell them they were going to call the police if they stayed in the building. I had one guy ask for a photo with me and [he] proceeded to feel my butt. The disrespect, hate, and stress involved in politics really make me wonder about subjecting my family to it, and although I find [public service] honorable, I wonder if it is worth it.

Her road signs that were placed on the roads were either destroyed or damaged with paint or smut graffiti. This is Canada?

Early Laws that Started the Shift

During Herbert Hoover's presidency, Andrew Mellon was appointed as secretary of state. Mellon was also DuPont's main investor and was himself the owner of many first resources or products that could be used by DuPont and easily marketed to the public. His nephew Harry Anslinger was appointed as head of the new Federal Bureau of Narcotics and Dangerous Drugs. Anslinger was a racist who hated Mexicans and was always looking for ways to confront them or threaten them. For him, making marijuana illegal was a dream weapon to hurt the Mexicans, who were recognized as extensive users and traffickers of the drug.

Secret meetings were held by corporation tycoons, including John D. Rockefeller and J. Paul Getty, and many other robber barons, and they all agreed that hemp was a menace to their empires of oil, cotton, forestry, and steel and had to be eliminated as a competitor if their dynasties were to remain intact and profitable. An obscure Mexican slang word for the plant was chosen. The word *marijuana* was adopted and, by way of clever media manipulation, was pushed onto the American consciousness. Had those captains of industry used the word *hemp*, it would have been considered a joke as everyone knew what hemp was and the many ways in which the plant was useful. The robber barons could never get away with banning hemp, and that is why they pushed this name that Americans did not know or care about, *marijuana*.

In the 1930s people did not much question the policies being introduced by governments and relied mostly on newspapers and radio to form an opinion. You would think that today, a ban on hemp would not pass unnoticed and there would be much debate, and it is doubtful if such a bill would see the light of day. But such a bill was in fact presented by Robert Doughton, strong supporter of the DuPont Corporation. It was presented via Doughton and the only committee that could introduce a bill to the floor without its being debated by other committees. On April 14, 1937, Congress passed the Prohibitive Marihuana Tax Law that outlawed marijuana, including hemp without any kind of opposition. This, of course, eliminated the competition of a product superior to the resources the robber barons owned or controlled such as oil, timber, concrete, cotton, and beef, among many others. Hemp had been used and manufactured into many useful products without much impact on the environment. It was totally renewable and easily transformed at a much lower cost than steel, concrete, combustibles, and most other products controlled by the likes of Rockefeller and Getty.

In the late 1920s and 1930s, media started pushing what was called "yellow journalism," which is the publication of articles with catchy headlines without much research in order to secure mainstream attention. They did not fail, and shortly afterward, the public opinion was cast. It was clear to the public that marijuana was dangerous, and everyone was aware that strong government action would be necessary— thus began the first-known US War on Drugs.

Newspapers were pumping fantastic stories with catchy and scary headlines to demonstrate the horrors of the new enemy: marijuana. The menace of marijuana made headlines everywhere.

The so-called evil plant was blamed for everything from car accidents, to loss of morality, to murder, and was supposed to render one dumb, stupid, and totally unfit to function in a normal, virtuous, and responsible society.

Movies were produced such as *Reefer Madness* (1936), *Assassin of Youth* (1935), and *Marihuana, the Devil's Weed*. These effectively turned marijuana into an enemy as perceived by the population. These films depicted marijuana users as extremely violent, totally devoid of all moral worth, extremely dangerous, and crazy. Of course, there were subtle remarks made about Mexicans. The drug was declared more dangerous than heroin or cocaine as it was presented as being the destroyer of moral fiber in the United States. It was described as a violent narcotic that provoked incurable insanity and had soul-destroying effects on individuals who used it. The *Reefer Madness* movie ended with these bold words on the screen: TELL YOUR CHILDREN.

Dr. James Woodward, a physician and attorney, attempted to testify on behalf of the American Medical Association by stating that what these films called marijuana was just a strain of the family of *Cannabis sativa*, with remarkable medicinal value, but his efforts were to no avail. The public was never made aware of the distinctions between hemp and marijuana. The AMA had already recognized cannabis/marijuana as a medicine found in numerous healing products that had been sold for quite some time without known side effects. Dr. Woodward was pushed aside, and hemp was effectively banned along with marijuana. And since this was presented in such a timely manner, people did not realize what had happened. The ban is still in place to this day in the United States, where *Cannabis sativa* is illegal to grow, consume, or market, although some states have declared it legal without federal approval.

As the public saw it, Congress had banned hemp because it was classed in the same category as marijuana, which was presented as a violent and dangerous drug. Hemp does nothing more than act as an amazing resource to virtually any industry and any product. At that time, in the thirties, hemp was made mainly into plastics, oil, and paper. Farmers complained, but since there was no longer a market for hemp products, which were illegal, they soon switched to other crops such as cotton, which is more polluting and more expensive as a fiber to transform. At about the same time, governments started subsidizing farmers.

Here we are in modern-day times and we are beginning to realize that we are in serious trouble when it comes to how we treat our environment. The resources and practices we use today for energy and for product creation are very harmful and toxic, not just to our planet but also to us.

Despite the full awareness that hemp is an option that could transform how things are done on this planet, governments continue to ban the plant or else control it, like Canada does, and it is still often mistaken for marijuana thanks to misinformation that leverages the fact that marijuana and hemp belong to the same family of plants. Later we will look at how the restoration or liberalization of the culture of hemp could be one of the most important actions in our effort to stabilize the planet. It could also be an important factor in balancing the budget, easing tension and trade wars between countries, and especially restoring some of our freedoms as we have become servants to shortsighted leaders who only want us to continue playing their commercial and nationalistic games.

Some Suggestions

We must recognize that modern farming using chemicals, GMOs, antibiotics, and growth hormones for methods of massive production has provided people with an abundance of cheaper food for a long time and could probably continue to do so, except for one major flaw in the system: the food we eat is toxic. Just imagine what would happen if, because of the use of such chemicals, pesticides, herbicides, and GMOs, bees were to become extinct. Pollinators, although not listed as endangered species, are indeed endangered because of the use of pesticides. Pollinators are the most important forms of life on this planet as they are necessary in the process of food production. Clearly, we must get closer to nature, but corporations will not likely see it that way. The use of pesticides will probably continue for a long time without much opposition. No magic potions or remedies, including the culture of cannabis or reforestation, will nurse the planet back to health in the short term, but I would like to make a few suggestions that, if implemented, would probably help Earth in its fight to pollution and make life somewhat less stressing and less toxic. We should make noise about some of these suggestions and make our governments understand that we will tolerate nothing else than their best efforts in this new direction of having a lower carbon footprint, improved social consciousness, and a cleaner environment. Here are a few suggestions that could help:

- Stabilize the economy and avoid any further debt.
- Levy a standard tax on products and income for everybody, including corporations.
- Provide strong social services—but those in need should give back to the system according to their ability to do so.
- Never invade a country or go to war without first consulting the people with a referendum.
- Have a strong military centered on defense.
- Invest in education.
- Divorce government from corporations.
- Divorce government from religion.
- Gradually replace our current energy system with one with an emphasis on renewable energy.
- Completely overhaul the pharmaceutical industry and medicine. Do more research on alternative healing and ancient healing techniques instead of masking symptoms with drugs and chemicals.
- Stop money laundering through real estate.
- Provide help to citizens of other troubled countries while proceeding with more caution before granting asylum to newcomers.
- Produce food locally and help small farmers to produce nontoxic foods.
- Give people their right to privacy.
- Have good pensions and retirement systems.

- Encourage people to grow their own food whenever possible.
- Return to the system of one citizen, one vote.
- Legalize the culture and transformation of hemp.
- Get out and *vote*.

While many of these suggestions have little to no chance of being implemented under the present regimes, it is up to us citizens to elect persons who are compatible with the planetary view and who are most likely to serve the people first. Note that the right to vote may in a near future become restricted to the point of being highly selective, meaning that elections would be a simple formality with their outcomes manipulated as is the case in many countries today. Western democracies are in a serious political crisis from which they may not recover.

We are inarguably on a path that is leading to self-destruction, even without considering the effects of earth's cycles, and unless we make a radical shift in human consciousness, we will encounter more serious troubles, some of which have already started. It is not difficult to evaluate the depressing results of our present actions and system. Here is a question that is not difficult to answer: How many generations will be able to thrive or even survive with the legacy we are leaving them, especially if we continue traveling the same destructive path we are now on?

The evolution of collective consciousness of our actions is a must. Our toxic level of fear, which engenders violence, has to be lowered or transcended, but this will not happen through administrative measures, military or police actions, religious interventions, oil wars, or any other such means, as such things create more problems than they solve as they are the control tools of the ruling class.

Of course, those who have a vested interest in protecting the status quo will not be silenced easily and will continue to spread fear, violence, and control. Everyone should realize that there are people who are now clinging to the belief that it is possible to enjoy a life of abundance, freedom, and prosperity if only they change their way of thinking, choose a different kind of commitment, and put forth the necessary effort to perceive the world in a different way.

There is a great deal of progress being made as we are collectively becoming more and more aware of our dual nature and our purpose for experiencing life on this planet. Despite some evidence to the contrary, we are becoming less dependent on religions and more spiritualized. We are now asking questions about how we can achieve a balance between our two seemingly opposed natures. Our media and ego-dominated system only lets us see the dark side of life, presenting images and stories of things such as war, catastrophe, poverty, and disease, but a little research will convince us that this world is filled with good people doing good deeds.

Fighting the dragon face-to-face will accomplish nothing except more of the same in the form of retaliations. The dragon must be defeated. This is clearly the work and duty of enlightened and brave individuals like you. The dragon must be tamed from within!

Please note that the preceding chapters are not meant to encourage consumption of marijuana. I personally have never consumed it and would not recommend it to anyone as I consider it a dangerous drug that can cause many problems for users and society.

The age of interrogation has been a long one. We have now come to the period of response.

What Is at Stake Here?

The earth, our mother, is a sacred garden in which
we have been granted the privilege to live. It seems
that we have lost sight of what we have done to it, and
we are now reaping the consequences of our actions.

During the period between World War II and 9/11, we
did not show much concern for the planet's ability
to renew the resources we were harvesting, and we
did not try hard to develop alternative methods of producing
goods and energy. During this long period of prosperity,
governments and corporations were reaping huge profits by
exploiting these natural resources. They also kept polluting
the ecosystem without consideration of even cleaning up after
their operations ceased.

While Earth is truly a living entity, it does not have the level of
consciousness that would give it the ability to limit the number
of humans and other life-forms allowed to live on its surface
or to limit the amount of resources being harvested. What
it does, however, is react to conditions in very definite ways
and according to immutable the natural laws it is submitted
to. Nowhere do we find a better exemplification of the old
expression "You reap what you sow" than in the working
mechanisms of Mother Earth. We have our planet down for
the count, and it will react according to basic natural and
eternal laws.

Without trying to sound alarmist, I will say that most of
us now realize that the state of our environment will not
permit us to continue in the direction we are heading, which
appears to be irreversible without serious modifications in
our present lifestyle. We have an urgent need to consider a

different approach to environmentalism. It is no longer about making the result of our actions more sustainable, despite our destructive industrial system, but is about transforming the human relationship with the earth and all life on it.

Activist communities, grassroots movements, and other organizations are fighting desperately to save what is left of our natural resources and wildlife, but not much will change unless we as humans reconsider our relationship with Mother Earth and our true place on the earth and within the universe.

Our history is abundant with stories of civilizations that have disappeared, sometimes without a trace, leaving us to wonder what could have happened to them. The Maya civilization is a good example of this. There are many videos and documentaries on this subject that try to determine the most probable causes for the disappearance of these past civilizations. Without jumping to conclusions, it can be reasonably assumed that the problem that led to their disappearance was the destruction of their living environment and overuse of their resources.

We are now facing the same problems ancient civilizations had to deal with, but this time, with the advent of mobility, instant communication, and globalization, we have spoiled the entire surface of the planet, polluted its water resources, changed the composition of the air we breathe and harvested more of the earth's natural resources than it has the ability to replace in the short time we impose on its regenerative process. We are harvesting natural resources at an alarming rate which could cause of a partial or total collapse of our eco-system.

It is not within the scope of *A Wall of Hate* to provide computer models of what could happen in the future or to make predictions as to what might happen to life on earth as we know it if we refuse to change the way we treat the planet. These subjects are amply and scientifically documented, and anything I could add would be for the most part guesswork or redundant. Globalization is still with us and is responsible for the attack on the whole planet's resources, but we see no point in wasting our efforts to oppose it, as trade wars and protectionism should turn the clock back to a time when countries were producing their own goods.

This is about something different. Here I make no attempt to convince anyone to give up all or part of their comforts, and I will not use the cliché that we should reduce, reuse, and recycle in order to leave a clean environment for future generations, as I am conscious that a good number of people are only paying lip service to this.

The way planet Earth is reacting to the present crisis is, in a lot of ways, predictable. It would not come as a surprise if there were a partial or total collapse of the system in the not-too-distant future. We know that humans and wildlife can adapt to changing conditions, but the question is, can we do it fast enough? For example, the North Pole's glaciers, the world's largest water resources, are melting at an alarming rate, which could leave us with considerably reduced freshwater supplies—and the amount of methane released in the atmosphere from a warmer climate melting the permafrost may turn out to be one of the tipping factors. This is a vicious circle: As more of the sun's radiation is absorbed by the warming earth and seawater, less energy is being reflected back into the stratosphere, thereby melting old glaciers, whose water ends up in the sea and is no longer usable as fresh or potable water unless it goes through a tedious process of filtration and desalination.

Back in 1963 while serving in the Canadian military, I was assigned to a posting in Churchill, Manitoba, where Canadian forces worked in collaboration with a US detachment from Cape Canaveral who were conducting research into the phenomenon of the northern lights. At that time, I performed a few experiments of my own and found that in the middle of summer, when the top part of the tundra melted beneath the sun, if you were to disturb the soil and light a match, the methane would start to burn and sometimes, with the help of the local Inuit, had to be controlled. This was more than fifty years ago. I have not returned to Hudson Bay since that time. But from documentaries and published reports, we can see that the tundra is now melting to the point where buildings that were sitting on permafrost are moving and will probably have to be destroyed or relocated. The whole system of roads and transportation built on permafrost is in a state of near collapse, especially in the summer months. The tree line, which was at the time near Thompson, Manitoba, has moved north about seventy-five miles. This means that huge amounts of methane and other gases are being released in the atmosphere, and the CO_2 produced by this phenomenon could, in the future, dwarf our own vehicle emissions. Hopefully the extra trees that will eventually cover the northern part of the Precambrian shield will absorb some of that CO_2 and release oxygen as they grow, and perhaps counteract some of the damage caused by the thinning of the ozone layer that covers the North Pole and the Arctic. There are now news reports that uncontrollable fires are burning in these regions, and scientists are concerned about the unprecedented increase in temperatures in the northern half of the globe and the fact that glaciers are melting at an unprecedented rate.

Our Planet's Reaction to Overharvesting

Planet Earth is the product of creation of some kind. Whether you believe it was created by a central intelligence we generally call God or you believe that everything we can observe in the universe happened by accident does not change the fact that the universe is there and that it conforms to very specific laws. Our beliefs, whatever they may be, will not change the laws, nor will they modify one iota the way they operate. This is not meant to start an argument between the believers and the atheists, but just the fact that the universe exists implies, first, creation and second, evolution. It is in fact difficult to think that a universe that obeys such precise and complex laws could have come about by accident and evolved by sheer necessity.

Our planet obeys one great law: that of cause and effect. It does not take much imagination to portray the effects of the law of gravity. If we throw a rock or solid object in the air, it will eventually fall back down, and if we remain in its path, its downward trajectory, then we are likely to learn a great lesson about gravity's effects. We will remember the results of setting this law in motion, and we will likely use more caution when dealing with gravity in the future. When we discuss karma in a later chapter, we will see that everything in the universe, including humankind, is subject to this law. This law does not seek revenge or impose punishment upon us for improper actions. Its workings and actions are impersonal and are simply the effects that must necessarily follow actions. Once we recognize and use the law of karma to our advantage, we will find it can be one of the greatest tools in the process of our evolution, both on the personal level and the planetary level. At this time it may be easy to conclude that climate change is the result of our actions, and this conclusion is probably true, at least for the most part, but global warming could also be attributed, in part, to the cycles the earth submits to in its journey through space. These cycles are discussed and presented in the book *Earth Fights Back*.

Let's look at some of the ways the planet reacts to definite causes. First, the planet, after establishing an orbit around the sun according to the definite law of attraction and repulsion between opposed polarities, in its molten mass, reacted to the heat from the sun but also to the cold that permeated its surroundings. Because of the presence of oxygen and hydrogen, present as gases, the earth naturally reacted by producing the phenomenon of humidity or water. This water, in turn, because of a reaction to heat and dryness, started to solidify and gave rise to earth in its most fundamental form of mixed liquid and solid elements. Because of the presence of these elements and their reaction to each other, a crust started to form, and the elements separated themselves according to their respective atomic weight and nature. The reaction of the new elements with each other and to the life force that is present everywhere gave birth to plant life, which started to separate some of the oxygen from the hydrogen and produced what we now know as air. No doubt you can anticipate my next statements. The process described in the Bible as the six days of creation could very well be the origin of the four basic elements beloved by ancient and modern alchemists, earth, water, air, and fire, which are considered to be the base for all transformations and transmutations when submitted to the four conditions of heat, humidity, coldness, and dryness. The alchemists did not believe these to be the only elements. Detractors later used this fact to discredit alchemy by claiming that the alchemists were therefore very simplistic and primitive minds. These detractors and modern scientists unknowingly use the same principles practiced by the alchemists with or without the knowledge that they were right.

Let's examine the way earth reacts to conditions. When a giant volcano erupts, the air becomes charged with toxic particles, which obscure the light of the sun, which in turn causes temporary minor or major climate changes that are felt around the globe. Our media immediately saturate the people with abundant information and overstatements, and silly as this may sound to some of us, they call it an act of God.

Earth does not react to the volcano, which is the cause, but to the lower amount of sunlight. The volcano, which is the cause of the disturbance, does not consciously erupt to punish anyone but is subject to the force of very definite pressures that make it erupt at a certain time and under certain conditions. It is certainly not the work of an elderly gentleman with a long white beard sitting on a cloud somewhere up there!

Suppose, for example, we consciously or unconsciously dump millions of tons of pollutants into the atmosphere. The planet will not go into a fury, put up its dukes, and start fighting back; it will simply react to the condition to which it has been submitted. Because of the pollution, the delicate balance of the earth's systems is modified. As a consequence, the thin layer of air surrounding the planet we call the atmosphere becomes charged with particles, partly blocking the sun and trapping some of its energy, which is then not reflected back in space but which generates extra heat on the solid surface of the earth.

If the planet were in perfect health, then trees and vegetation would rapidly absorb this extra carbon in the atmosphere and in turn produce oxygen that would clean up the air without causing any dangerous reactions. Since almost 70 percent of the original tree cover has been harvested or destroyed with previous forests turned into deserts, the remaining trees will absorb a portion of the gases and contribute to the restoration of the earth's balance but will be unable to absorb enough of these gases to make much of a difference. The air that is not cleaned remains charged with particles, thereby causing further deterioration of the air quality, and in a sort of vicious circle, it traps energy from the sun, further upsetting the balance. This is a very simplistic and unscientific explanation of some of the causes of global climate change, but whatever the case may be, we will have to adapt, and this in a short time, to the changes taking place on the planet.

For our purpose, we will accept the data available from scientists and organizations who have conducted such research. The point is to inform our readers that if we are to nurse our planet back to health, it will be necessary to reduce the damage we are inflicting on the planet and, among other things, plant trees or regreen the planet on a massive scale to restore some kind of balance. And we must certainly reinstate the growth of hemp as a way of reducing our dependence on petroleum, forests, and mining products.

The damage done to planet Earth is serious but not irreversible. We, as a global species, now realize that something must be done. Already some countries have taken bold action by electing governments and administrations dedicated to the reversal of the present trend, where business is based solely on excessive profits and overconsumption, and to working with other countries to try to control the damage we are inflicting on the planet. This is going to be a rough ride for these courageous individuals as they are not promoting hatred, greed, and division but are working with principles of cooperation and tolerance. Large corporations that have been reaping natural resources for bargain basement prices, often subsidized by the taxpayers for taking these resources without much regard for the environment are not likely to easily relinquish their power to do so. Probably the most potent weapon we have at our disposal is public opinion. If enough people are convinced that something can be done, then public opinion will eventually prevail. As a matter of fact, public opinion is prevailing at this time as the majority of us want money, power over others, and almost unlimited consumer goods, and we use this derived power for our own well-being where the acquisition of abundant goods determines one's standing within the community.

It is evident that a large proportion of people have adopted an aggressive and hateful lifestyle without realizing that this is the very essence of what creates wars. In many ways, we are not so different from the pre–World War II Nazis in the respect that we direct our hatred toward individuals or to segments of our own population whom we perceive as different or undesirable.

Some of the Solutions Applied by Right-Wing Governments Could Be Potentially Good for the Environment

As out of place as this may seem, some of the actions now taken by right-wing governments are or could be great assets in reestablishing some kind of balance in our ecosystem by drastically reducing the amount of goods being produced while maintaining the population at a sustainable level and with a manageable degree of obedience. These proposed solutions may not be popular, but they have the potential to achieve some of the changes considered necessary. Ironically, some governments fiercely oppose the implementation of a carbon tax and even produce trash ads leading us to believe that they have better solutions—and they may be right in some of their claims. Some of these policies include such things as the following:

1. **Drastic cuts in the education system.** These cuts will affect mostly low-income families who will not be able to educate their children, which will decrease budget expenses for the government. This goes hand in hand with minimum wage cuts for students. Uneducated youngsters will work for less money and will have no choice as many other temporary benefits are also being chopped. This will also provide the government with a great tool for dealing with the problem of immigration and racism. Uneducated people work for less and are easier to control and manipulate. This will also provide a large pool of available workers whom corporations can count on. The constant devaluation of the purchasing power of currencies will also contribute to many students' not being able to continue or get an education.

2. **Keeping the poor off the road.** Manipulation of combustible prices will guarantee that low-income citizens will have no choice but to reduce their travel expenses since these increases will affect not only transportation but also necessary heating in the winter and will raise the price of all that is produced with petroleum products. Government can collect more taxes while reducing the amount of energy produced, an environmental plus.

3. **Cuts in municipal handouts.** This one is not a direct hit, but it will force municipalities to cut services and raise property and other taxes or implement user fees, thereby cutting back the costs while maintaining the same level of government.

4. **Opposing or fighting environmental projects.** This one is serious and will affect the way all levels of government interact. It even entails a real possibility of a total breakdown of communications between governments, which could possibly lead to a breakup of a country, leading to fewer goods being produced and less resources being harvested.

5. **Severe cuts to health care.** The effect of these cuts will be to provide reduced services in all areas of the health-care system with longer waiting periods and a shortage of qualified professionals. This in turn will shorten the life span of many elderly people who have become or will soon become dependent on the system.

6. **Deep cuts to welfare programs,** which will force many recipients to do without or to look for other solutions, leaving the government with a reduced welfare budget and the possibility of reducing administrative staff.

It is claimed that, and as we can see, the carbon tax is not the only way to protect the environment. This is probably right considering actions already taken by the Ontario government, for example. The question is, will they reduce spending and downsize the government accordingly? Cutting back on the minimum wage for workers while granting large increases in salary and benefits for the elected or appointed officials of their party are indications of the direction they will likely take. Despite claims that they are working for the people, they are really working for themselves and the corporations that put them in power, while the population is being lulled to sleep by fancy talk and claims about the government working for "we the people."

Even if these measures would be favorable to the environment, whatever benefits gained stand a good chance of being redirected as additional profits for those in command.

Are We Ready for Solutions?

The Paris Conference

The Paris Conference on climate change that was held in December 2015 was probably a giant step in the right direction, but overall self-interests prevailed. China pledged only what it was supposed to have been doing in the first place, because of pressure from its own citizens who want to see the sun shining and breathe cleaner air with the accompanying freedom to walk in the open without the aid of a face mask.

Although on the surface the conference looked promising, and even though all participants signed the pledges (yes, even Russia and China), there is no mechanism in place to enforce the directives. It will take a long time before we find out if the pledges have been honored. This leaves a lot of room for variables, changes, manipulations, and cancellations. The conference therefore had the virtue of appeasing the masses, who probably thought that something worthwhile and promising had been accomplished, but any favorable outcomes will depend heavily on the goodwill of the governing powers and their willingness to allocate the funds for these environmental programs.

The new buzzword that came out of this conference was *sustainability*. One does not have to be a scientist to realize that true sustainability is not likely to be attained with the present pledges, even if they are followed to the letter. On the one hand we are asking that something be done to save the planet, while on the other, we still demand that our economies show constant annual growth while corporations continue to run the show. Sustainability is impossible to achieve forever on a planet with limited resources unless there is a shift toward cleaner energies and renewable resources. If we are to have any kind of impact on the quality of our environment, there will have to be a decrease in the amount of carbon being released and an increase in the amount of oxygen being produced.

There probably will be an increase in the number of automobiles and other manufactured goods that will cancel any advantages we may have gained, but keep in mind that electric and hybrid vehicles are likely to form a good part of the transportation sector in the not too distant future, which will reduce the amount of fossil fuels being burned. It is interesting that all present at the Paris Conference were in favor of a carbon tax. Some of the countries are now in the process of implementing such a tax. The government of Canada has already announced its own implementation of a carbon tax on gasoline and other items. While the central government implemented such a tax, there is a struggle between the federal and provincial governments to determine who should or could apply or enforce it. Ontario originally refused to implement the tax within the province. The provinces will likely claim that they have rights and jurisdiction over natural resources within their own territories. The tax is already in effect in Canada and seems to favor the population and the diminishing middle class over corporations.

A scenario that we could applaud is a system where a green tax is collected and put into a special account with the funds allocated to reforestation projects, local organic hydroponic farming projects, cleanup of our rivers, land reclamation, and other green endeavors. Some of these funds could also be devoted to research into alternative energy development to produce cleaner fuels to run our cars with. The new Canadian carbon tax system meets a good portion of these criteria.

You may think by now that the author has probably lost it as we are not even near the point of developing new and cleaner fuels, slowing down the deforestation process, or finding more environment-friendly materials to use in manufacturing, thereby slowing down mining and other destructive ways of harvesting the natural resources of the planet. The startling truth is, as they say, "Been there, done that." It is a fact that at one time, cleaner fuels were developed and used. Automobile prototypes were developed with minimal use of steel and glass that were cheaper to build and, as a bonus, were easily biodegradable. Henry Ford developed such a car; there is ample documentation of this. Ford is shown in a video dated 1942 with a car he had built with hemp that was ten times as strong as steel. In fact, he is shown hitting the body of the car with a sledgehammer without even making a dent on its surface. This car also ran on oil derived from hemp and soy. The first engines built by Rudolf Diesel ran on clean fuel made from hemp, easily obtainable and cheaply produced, until hemp was declared illegal. Reinstating the culture and transformation of hemp, while not the only solution, would go a long way toward the preservation of our forest, drastic reductions in the production of fossil fuels, and a like reduction in the amount of steel required to build vehicles and other goods. Surprisingly, the money given as grants and benefits to oil companies would pay for the transition from carbon-based to renewable energies.

A Short History of Hemp

Throughout the history of the world, hemp has been cultivated and used for many purposes and has proven to be one of the most valuable plants we have at our disposal. Following is a timeline presenting some of the historical facts about hemp:

4000 BC. Clay pot unearthed in Taiwan decorated with wrapped hemp wire.

2800 BC. Egyptian goddess Sashat portrayed with a hemp leaf over her head. Hemp was used at that time to make rope, medicine, and clothing.

2600 BC. Chinese emperor Shennong's first medical text found outlining the healing virtues of hemp.

2000 BC. Ancient Hindu transcript lists dried hemp leaves, seeds, and stems in medical texts.

1500 BC. Cannabis is listed as medicine in the Ebers Papyrus from ancient Egypt.

200 BC. First paper invented in China, made from hemp.

AD 70. Roman emperor Nero lists hemp extract in medical text that was used for over one thousand years.

AD 400. Mummified Yingpan man unearthed wearing a painted mask made of hemp. This is probably the first known hemp bioplastic.

1454. Gutenberg Bible, the world's first typeset book, printed on hemp paper.

1492. Christopher Columbus brings European hemp to the New World.

1533. King Henry VIII issues a royal proclamation imposing fines on farmers who do not grow hemp.

1538. England botanist William Turner praises hemp as the most amazing medicine in his book *New Herbals*.

1619. The United States' first cannabis law orders that all farmers *must* grow hemp. Hemp was accepted as legal tender for payment of taxes.

1690. First US paper mill makes paper from hemp.

1763. New law in the United States makes growing hemp compulsory for farmers.

1776. Declaration of Independence written on hemp paper by a hemp farmer.

1789. "Make the most of hemp seed. Sow it everywhere," said George Washington.

1801. "Hemp is of first necessity to the wealth and protection of the country. If people let the government decide what food to eat, [what] medicine to take, their bodies will soon be in as sorry a state as are the souls of those who live under tyranny," said Thomas Jefferson, president of the United States and hemp farmer.

1853. Levi Strauss, based in the United States, creates world's first pair of jeans, made of hemp.

1897. Rudolph Diesel invents the first diesel engine that runs on hemp oil, which causes very little pollution and does not create carbon buildup in engines. Hemp oil was his natural choice of fuel until it was made illegal.

1930. Henry Anslinger appointed commissioner of the newly created Federal Bureau of Narcotics by his father-in-law, Andrew Mellon, one of the most powerful bankers in the USA. Mellon and two other bankers, John D. Rockefeller and Andrew Carnegie, had significant investments in oil, paper, synthetic fiber, petrochemical, plastics, and pharmaceuticals, all of which could have been made obsolete by technological advancements in hemp processing. So they launched a PR campaign to demonize hemp and used Anslinger to trick the public into believing that any and all cannabis was a dangerous drug that was killing American teenagers and causing black people and Mexicans to commit sex crimes against white American women.

1937. The US Congress approves a bill that prohibits the cultivation of all cannabis, including hemp.

1938. *Popular Mechanics* magazine article titled "New Billion-Dollar Crop" announces the arrival of the new hemp processing technology that was set to make hemp the United States' #1 commodity had it not been prohibited.

1939. The then mayor of New York City did not believe the anti-cannabis propaganda. He commissioned thirty-one independent scientists to undertake a five-year scientific investigation into the physical effects of consuming cannabis. The results revealed that cannabis does not cause aggressive or antisocial behavior, does not cause an increase in sexual depravity, and does not alter the fundamental aspects of one's personality. The US government started a nationwide search to locate and burn all copies of the document to prevent the public from finding out that they had been deceived.

1941. Henry Ford asks, "Why use up the forests which were centuries in the making and the mines which required ages to lay down if we can get the equivalent of forest and mineral products in the annual growth of the hemp fields?"

Ford had built a car almost entirely from hemp that ran on clean-burning hemp fuel. The car was 30 percent lighter than its metal counterpart, and the body was many times stronger and much more resistant than metal. These cars never were put into production because hemp was by then illegal, and Ford, like Diesel, had to follow suit and abandon hemp as a viable alternative to steel and oil in building and fueling cars.

1956. The US government elevates the classification of cannabis to a Schedule 1 narcotic, defining it as having no medicinal value and as being as harmful as cocaine and heroin. Anyone found in possession of cannabis, including hemp plants, could face life imprisonment.

1961. Henry Anslinger attends the United Nations and exerts power over the UN to have cannabis cultivation prohibited in 150 countries worldwide. The results of this is that most of the world's food, fuel, medicine, and fiber goes from being grown organically by farmers to being produced chemically under the control of the pharmaceutical and petrochemical industries. It took only a few decades to plunge the world into a toxic ecological catastrophe that worsens each year.

1975. The US government funds research in Virginia and discovers that cannabis can reverse the effects of cancer and destroys cancerous cells. The study is stopped, and it is determined that future research into cannabis as related to cancer will be prohibited.

1996. Canada legalizes the growing of hemp, which creates jobs and revenues, but the industry remains highly regulated and controlled.

2011. Kestrel, a car made of hemp, is unveiled. With a range of 160 km (100 miles) and a weight of 2,500 lb. It was named the eco-friendliest car in the world. The car was never put into production, but there seems to be other experimental projects in producing vehicles made of hemp and/or other plants. This of course cannot be confirmed as there is no official documentation. It is based solely on what is presented on the internet.

2015. During the electoral campaign in 2015, Justin Trudeau, the Liberal candidate for the position of prime minister, makes an electoral promise to legalize marijuana in Canada with the help and consent of the provinces. This project has now been implemented, and it is no longer a crime to use recreational marijuana, which is no longer classified as a dangerous drug.

It is to be noted that the use of recreational marijuana, while being legal, is tightly regulated and controlled. Governments can sell the product, but illegal distributors and users could face severe penalties for violations. Let's note also that although hemp can be legally grown in Canada, there is still a mountain of side regulations and red tape that prevents the culture of cannabis plants by anyone other than currently government-approved volume producers. An application for a license must be submitted. The request is then evaluated, and if it is found suitable, the applicant is directed to purchase the seeds from currently approved growers, the only source available. The permit is issued on a yearly basis. Hemp seeds can be purchased legally over the counter as a nutritional supplement, but the producer sterilizes the seeds according to government regulation by boiling them before offering them for sale to prevent germination. Growers are not allowed to sell the leaves or stems of the plant to the public. Hopefully, with a new government that seems to be open to different solutions, there should be liberalization and a decrease in the red tape that discourages farmers wishing to grow, transform, or sell their crops. Ideally, government would support the industry. This could be the beginning of a new era as the culture, harvesting and transformation of plants would create jobs that are so much needed while assisting governments in the task of balancing a budget and be a tremendous asset to environmental programs. In Canada government approved volume growers can legally plant hemp seeds but not the average farmer.

Some Facts about Hemp

Hemp can be made into fine-quality paper, using eighty five percent fewer chemicals than the varieties made of wood fiber, and this, without the use of chlorine bleach. It is also recyclable more times than wood fiber paper.

Hemp can grow well in a wide variety of soils and temperatures without the need for pesticides or herbicides.

It can be used to restore soil contaminated by oils, chemicals, and radioactive spills.

Each acre of hemp leaves about four tons of stems that can be transformed into building materials or blocks that can easily replace cement or concrete.

An acre of hemp produces four times the fiber of the average acre of forest over a period of twenty years.

An acre of hemp can absorb four times the CO_2 and produce four times the amount of oxygen than an acre of forest over a period of twenty years.

Crops can be rotated easily with others such as corn and cotton, restoring the depleted soil in the process.

Of the Medicinal Virtues of Cannabis Seeds

Seeds of the hemp plant contain all the essential amino acids and essential fatty acids necessary to maintain healthy human life. No other single plant source provides complete protein nutrition in such an easily digestible form. More importantly, hemp seed contains the oils essential to life in the perfect ratio for human health and vitality. Hemp seed oil (35 percent of total seed weight) is the richest source in the plant kingdom of these essential fatty acids (EFAs). The lustrous oil contains 80–81 percent EFAs and is among the lowest in saturated fat content at 8 percent of total oil volume. Marijuana seeds are nature's perfect food for humanity.

Biochemist Dr. R. Lee Hamilton said, "The EFAs are responsible for our immune system." She, along with fellow UCLA researcher William Eidleman, conducted promising research using the EFAs in the treatment of AIDS-related immune deficiency. In an open letter concerning the valuable hemp seed released by the two researchers (December 29, 1991), they announced that the possibility of feeding the world "is at our fingertips" and went on to state, "What is the richest source of essential oils? Yes, you guessed it, the seeds from the cannabis hemp plant. What better proof of the life-giving values of the now illegal seed? What the world needs now is intelligent relegalization of cannabis hemp, especially for medical intervention." (Dr. R. Lee Hamilton)

Studies done by seven-time Nobel Prize nominee Dr. Johanna Budwig have shown unparalleled results in the use of EFAs in the treatment of terminal cancer patients. In her book *Flax Oil as a True Aid against Arthritis, Heart Infraction, Cancer, and Other Diseases*, Dr. Budwig indicates that a balanced diet of essential fatty acids would keep our cells biologically electron rich. Saturated fats and trans fats, contained in most of the food oils we now use, alter the electronic charge of the unsaturated oils in cell membranes, decreasing the cells' ability to store and receive electrons from the sun. Budwig goes on to quote quantum physicist Friedrich Dessauer: "If it were possible to increase the concentration of solar electrons tenfold in this biological electron rich molecule, people could to some degree, increase their life span."

Like prophets in ages past, Dr. Budwig's revelation of truth threatened the ambitions of the high priests of commercialism. In her case, these were high priests of commerce controlling science for profit. Dr. Budwig ran afoul of the powerful corporations that process food oils when she discovered that fatty substances in soft tumors contained polymerized fats of marine animal origin. These polymers are formed when highly unsaturated fish and whale oils are heated to very high temperatures. She knew these oils were used in partially hydrogenated fat that cannot be made without high temperatures.

The director of the institute where she worked had financial interests in margarine and held patents on its manufacture, including the hydrogenation processes that produced the toxic polymers Budwig had found in tumors. He was afraid her discoveries would ruin margarine sales. He offered her money and ownership of a drugstore to keep her quiet. But

Dr. Budwig refused to be bribed and in her official capacity made public statements warning people of the possible health hazards of consuming margarine.

She was cut off from access to her laboratory. She was prevented from using research facilities at other institutes, and she could not get any more of her papers published in the fat research journals. This was astonishing because she had worked in collaboration with several hospitals, plus she held a high government post. It was her official responsibility to monitor the effects of drugs and processed foods on health.

Dr. Budwig courageously fulfilled her public duty in the face of opposition from food oil companies and threats to her career. She left the government position in 1953 and opened a clinic where she has successfully treated cancer patients by way of nutritional therapy. Because this great woman was blackballed by the greed of food oil companies, EFA research has been slowed for over thirty years. Current investigations are merely following in her footsteps. She also conducted intensive research on the medical virtues of plants, especially cannabis.

The United States government has been allowing the import of hemp seeds as long as they are steam sterilized at 212°F to prevent the possibility of sprouting. That temperature does not ruin the EFAs, though it does somewhat uncoil the highly nutritious protein in the seeds. Now that hemp seed consumption has increased dramatically in the United States, the federal government has decreed that the seeds must be dry heated to over 300°F, causing the EFAs to denature and become toxic. (Some states have already legalized the culture of hemp. The central government may also be considering action in that direction.)

While hemp may not be the all-encompassing solution to all our present problems, the shift to extensive hemp farming would ease the pressure on natural resources so much so that the countries that have been in debt and at war since the beginning of the Industrial Revolution could begin operating in the black and be able to devote a good portion of their resources to health, education, and the restoration of the ecosystem of the planet. Just consider a world where vehicles would run on clean-burning fuel. And as a bonus, this would eliminate the battles for oil monopolies where countries send their youths to fight each other in oil-related bloody wars. Most of our paper, cardboard, and plastics could be fabricated from the plant at a fraction of the cost of processing wood fibers or oil-derived products, and it would be biodegradable as a bonus. Although trees would still have to be harvested, a good portion of our forests could be saved and perhaps we could achieve real sustainability in the forestry sector—and as a bonus, we would stop some of the outrageous illegal logging.

Hemp would restore the contaminated soils, clean up the air, and provide us with numerous products such as food, clothing, powerful medicine, vehicles, fuel, and construction materials, among many others. Research is necessary to find out what the real potential of this one action could have on climate change, the economic woes, and the constant state of war we presently see in the world. This plant is probably the most useful gift that has been given to us by nature. Cultivating hemp on a massive scale could be the first important step in restoring our ecosystem and regaining some of the freedom that was taken from us.

Governments have been cooperating with the large and powerful corporations to include hemp with marijuana in the same category as a drug and it is time to set the records straight, even though the brainwashing will probably continue for a long time to come because, as it stands, we are threatening those corporations and governments with a drop in their profits and a loosening of their controls. Corporations will not change direction unless they can rake in big money in the process. It is up to us, "we the people," to roll up our sleeves and start exerting pressure on our leaders until they realize that legalizing hemp or releasing controls is an idea whose time has come.

The idea is not to kill the corporations but simply to reduce the power they are now enjoying and all the abuses they are involved in. This system which has given too much power to corporations has made slaves of the masses. Just remember back in the 1950s and 1960s when the family unit was still strong, when one person could make a good living and provide for the whole family, and this, without much of the stress attached to holding a job or even two jobs today, especially when both parents have to work to make ends meet. Despite claims that the economy is booming and that there are a record number of jobs available, most of these jobs are in the service sectors and are paid at such a low level that one would have to work at least two jobs in order to support a family. The advent of the new wave of overpaid CEOs centered on cutting costs and boosting production is enough to give anyone's mental health a good ride.

Releasing the hold that has been put on hemp would destroy some jobs but would create different and better ones—as many, if not more. Most hemp products could be produced locally, thereby easing the transfer of jobs to countries like China, India, and Afghanistan and reduce the dangerous number of trucks crowding the highways.

The cannabis plant has traditionally been revered as a plant that makes an impact on the agricultural, medicinal, and spiritual aspects of life. When it was outlawed, people were deprived of all the benefits associated with the plant. Some replaced it with crops that were more profitable to them.

In ancient times, the cannabis plant was considered a mind-altering substance used during religious initiations assisting candidates in achieving spiritual awareness. For this reason alone, it is no wonder that the hypermasculine, patriarchal, corporate government complex has decided to outlaw it. What is tragic is that hemp, which is of the same family of plants as marijuana but without any significant amount of the mind-altering chemical THC, was incorporated in the ban.

The foregoing statement should not be taken as support for the legalization of marijuana, considering the use that people make of it today. It is being consumed as a recreational drug, and those who indulge in it do so with the same attitude with which people approach the use of alcohol and consider it the equivalent of going on a binge with alcohol and/or other mind-altering substances. For that reason, it is dangerous. Yes, it can cause vehicle accidents, it is considered addictive for unstable individuals, and it can create financial hardship for people indulging in it, especially since the drug, being illegal, is grossly overpriced.

Yes, the culture of hemp should probably be given first priority, along with reforestation, as these two things could stabilize the economy in a relatively short period of time, create jobs, reduce the harvesting of our natural resources, and contribute to cleaner air while restoring formerly overused lands and providing us with many useful products, easy to manufacture, that will not end up on the stockpile of trash as most oil-derived products do.

Our Attitude toward the Environment

I n trying to determine the possibilities of restoring our planet to a state of health, I posed a few questions to random individuals of all classes, and the answers were almost the same and consistent in every case. Everyone interrogated wanted to leave a clean environment as a legacy to future generations. Most also unconditionally supported the protection of wildlife, regeneration of our forests, better management of natural resources, conservation, recycling, and all other actions that could leave our planet in a better state than it was in when we were born.

When questioned about their involvement or what they could or would do to help, most felt that the health of our planet was the responsibility of our elected officials. All were concerned about the state of our civilization where headlines of mass shootings are an almost daily occurrence and where global war is not merely a remote possibility but has become almost inevitable.

When, as individuals, we are making decisions concerning the state of the planet and the actions we should take to help the environment, we seem to separate the present from the reality future generations will be faced with. Everyone sincerely wished that all the environment-related problems we are aware of could be solved, along with the present nightmare of violence, gun use, murders, and suicides. When questioned further about what they would be willing to contribute to the effort of restoring the health of the planet, a good portion of those surveys did not answer or shied away from the subject. Some even said that it was too late and, therefore, a complete waste of time—and anyhow, even if they contributed, other people and other countries would continue with their devastating methods. They felt that their efforts would not amount to much anyway. Some became annoyed and even aggressive and would not discuss the topic any further. They even let me know that they considered environmentalists to be unrealistic daydreamers who perhaps should roll up their sleeves and start cleaning up the earth. Overall, we are generally concerned about the state of the planet and violence, but not enough to get involved in immediate personal action.

The Fears Associated with Change

Most people I surveyed are, if not wealthy, reasonably comfortable money-wise. The majority said that they had worked hard to acquire money and properties and wished to leave as much as possible to their families as their legacy. When asked which would choose between leaving a legacy to family and contributing to the efforts toward a cleaner environment, all said that leaving material possessions to their families was their main concern. When asked if they would support environmental projects, most responded with a resounding yes, but some became disturbed, anxious, and stressed, and a few expressed a fear of being dispossessed of their material possessions in the process of transforming the economy from carbon-based to renewable energies.

In the informal survey conducted among a group I am associated with the members' response was clear in that money was their first order of priorities in the pursuit of happiness. Their answers to the question showed priorities in this order:

1. Being rich.
2. Being in good health.
3. Being beautiful physically.
4. Being famous.

5. Being passionate about something.
6. Being intelligent.
7. Belonging to a close-knit family.
8. Working in an interesting occupation.
9. Loving someone.
10. Being loved by someone.
11. Contributing to the good of society.

Being rich was the number one choice. Note that my own answers were very similar to those given, except that, like those who have beaten the odds when facing serious medical conditions, I chose "being in good health" as my first concern. I changed my second choice from "being rich" to "being prosperous" because I do not wish to be involved in the soul-destroying process of amassing a fortune. Being frequently referred to as an environment freak, I had number eleven as my third choice.

People want to look first after their own interests, and this is how it is meant to be. There are, however, one fact we should be aware of, that a switch from a carbon to a renewable energy economy, would not only be in the individual's best interests but also would be good for our planet and society in general.

The switch from carbon-driven vehicles to hybrid or electric-powered vehicles, which has already started, proves to be a good change. We can already see great benefits coming from this change, and this without any disruption to our personal assets or the economy of the country we live in.

The switch from fossil fuel to renewable energy has also already started, and it could be the beginning of the recovery process for our planet, bringing with it the creation of real, much-needed jobs and opportunities.

As stated before, the reinstatement and liberalization of the culture of hemp could be one of the major factors in the process of recovery, creating countless opportunities for farmers and for logging contractors, who could become harvesters of an environmentally friendly product. Contractors and corporations will be needed to build transformation plants, creating good-paying jobs for the workers and many other benefits that are too numerous to list.

The transformation will not come without fierce opposition from corporations and governments, but in the end, we the people have the power to force such a shift and even those governments and corporations will reap its benefits. Politicians, in trying to get elected, often make statements about actions they intend to take, very often not realizing that once they get in power, they will have to recognize and deal with the real power behind the economy. This is the reason why so many electoral promises are broken. Our leaders are, for the most part, decent human beings who would certainly work with the people if there was enough pressure or the will to change. Even corporations may consider relinquishing some of their monopolies on natural resources and settle for reasonable profits if they were forced to. This would have to start with us, the shareholders, the workers, the small business owners, but businesses could be as profitable, if not more profitable, after the changes are in place.

Personal Power

The first and most important action required to break the wall of hate is to change the way we think, act, and speak. We must stop being cranky and start thinking for ourselves. This is not an easy task, but the benefits far outweigh the cost of our efforts. Cleaning our environment is not a sacrifice. It should be neither a burden nor an impossible dream. The process of rebuilding our society and restoring our home will not drive us to the poorhouse as some fearmongers would like us to believe.

First, we would have to stop participating in spreading the wave of hate by being at least neutral. We live in an extremely aggravating world where everything is accelerated, and we are constantly driven to act on impulse rather than reason. Discussing climate change without getting emotional is a difficult task because it cannot be mentioned without touching on political, religious, and corporate leaders and groups.

There is now an increasing awareness that our ego-centered system needs a complete overhaul and that there are no magical formulas that will suddenly raise the level of collective consciousness. The change will have to start with the individual.

The actions we take as individuals eventually transform into what we do collectively; this includes war, strife, hate, recessions, and, yes, harmony and peace. One does not have to turn into a saint or a hermit to accomplish great things for the collectivity. Granted, the results will not show until enough of us start thinking for ourselves. As soon as peace is mentioned, we revert to believing what we have been brainwashed to believe, namely that we each have to become a meek daydreamer who does not get involved in strife and who acts peacefully toward all humankind even if we are attacked or an act of violence is committed against us. Being peaceful and at ease with one's inner self in no way implies that one should submit or bend to the bullying practices used by what seems now to be a majority of the population supporting dictatorships, the likes of which have has invaded human relations for the past half century and is now steeply increasing, giving us a world that is exceedingly stressful and dangerous. Neither does being peaceful imply that one cannot defend himself or herself against attacks or violence. In fact, it is a responsibility and duty to protect oneself, one's family and property.

One may question what it is that has driven human beings throughout history. We are now on a hair-raising journey through time that is based on something probably as old as civilization itself like personal power, greed and an eternal thirst for domination over others. People who have mastered the art of commanding in the past have used it to acquire more than their share of wealth by any means, fair or foul can easily be traced and identified throughout history.

From the early tribal chieftains, to Alexander the Great, to Julius Caesar, and more recently the so-called robber barons and the emergence of superpowers, society and civilization has been shaped by individuals who have dared to be different and have mastered the art of commanding with confidence. The end results of their greed have always been wars, inquisitions, revolutions, crusades, massive genocides, and incredible suffering for so many.

In a globalized world such as we are living in now, it is obvious that we have failed to benefit from the lessons of history, accessible to both rulers and their populations, that should point the way toward a more friendly and civilized future. We know perfectly well what we are doing to the planet, but we still consider corporate profits above the survival of perhaps all species by making portions of, or all the earth inhabitable. We proudly point to the fact that modern society has extended the human life span considerably by developing a health-care system that is nothing short of amazing, technology that should make us freer, and a system of mass production of food never seen before. While the value of modern chemical farming who for a long time has supplied us with a surplus of food, is to be recognized, it is also true that there are flaws in the system that are beginning to translate into health problems, the elimination of pollinators, and depletion of soils. It is only a matter of time before chemicals will have to be abandoned and we will be forced to return to local farming for a healthy supply of nontoxic food.

History teaches us that after great, dominant and violent rulers disappeared from the face of the earth, there was a period of recovery with relative peace and healing. Many people relocated to new territories, but it will not to be the case this time around as the whole planet has been devastated almost beyond recognition and we have nowhere else to go.

I realize that it is the duty of a writer to inspire the readers and direct them toward a better way of life, but it is difficult to ignore the present situation and the fact that we are facing burdens and destructive conditions never experienced before. My hope is to inspire people to engage in self-development while still contributing to the well-being of society and looking for solutions.

One simple way we can make a serious contribution, actively participate in the process of regeneration and regain some of our freedom is by growing our own food, either individually or collectively.

To do nothing at this time is to accept the death sentence that has been handed to us.

The Wisdom of Nature

T he forest was shrinking, but the trees kept voting for the ax, for the ax was clever and had convinced the trees that, because it had a wooden handle, it was one of them.

To say that we have become disconnected from nature is an enormous understatement. We have become so concerned with our own survival in a jungle of hate, violence, and traffic that we would be at a loss to explain what nature is and how it works. But if we are to proceed with actions toward regulating the climate, we will first have to understand nature, what it really is and how it works, and from there take appropriate actions to rectify whatever we have done to cause nature's gradual and seemingly irreversible destruction.

The new generation so willing to fight climate change could consider nature as their first target and start working on positive changes that will make the old paradigms of the wall of hate obsolete. Protesting may be attention grabbing, but it will not accomplish much in the way of positive changes as retaliations will engender endless tit-for-tat situations with a highly favored, predictable, and almost inevitable winner: Big Brother.

I consider our present situation in relation to climate change to be a pressing emergency, and even though I still favor reforestation as one of the best methods in terms of healing the planet, trees take too long to grow back to make an immediate difference. There have been periods of climate change in the past, and some species have adapted, but because now the changes are rapidly accelerating, we may not have time enough to adapt to the many new conditions.

It would be fitting at this time to give a short presentation on how nature operates in the wild and how we have changed and modified natural patterns that have ruled our planet for millennia, replacing them with destructive man-made solutions based strictly on high productivity and profits.

Trees that grow in their own natural environment do so collectively, as in the case of conifers, which propagate generally from a cone that has been exposed to enough heat to open it up and release its seeds. Another method widely used by nature in the migration and expansion of forests is the transport of seeds from one area to another by way of birds, bears, and other animals through their feces. Fire, although destructive in the short term, is a great regenerator as it opens the cones of conifers and destroys the parasites that would choke young deciduous trees.

Conifers develop and grow an intricate web of roots, shallow and interlaced, that connects all the trees together. With the assistance of fungi, this enables them to store water and nutrients in plentiful quantities to survive a harsh winter or assist one of the trees in the network that may have been damaged. One other benefit to being so conveniently connected to each other is that it affords protection against high winds and storms. Whereas one tree along could not withstand high winds, the tree stand, united, connected, and with their roots interlaced, can withstand such winds without serious damage except for the breaking of limbs that were probably weak and drying anyway, thereby improving their collective health without spending energy on getting rid of those now useless limbs.

Nature automatically produces an intricate and almost unexplainable collection of pairs of predator and prey, from the humblest earthworm to the larger creatures that control each other's population and thereby maintain the delicate balance between animal species and plant life. The trees themselves develop their own protection against their enemies to a certain point, that is, until there is a disturbance of some kind in the balance between the bugs that attack them and their own predators.

It is not within the scope of *A Wall of Hate* to discuss at length and in detail the mysterious and precise work of nature, but I will give a short presentation on how a forest generally adapts itself to conditions depending on the number and nature of its parasites, its location, humidity, weather, and other factors influencing its growth, susceptibility to disease, or survival.

To develop and grow naturally, a forest depends on nutrients, which are generally present from the decomposition of trees from previous generations and the bodies of dead animals that were once part of the food chain of the forest. These were processed into feces (or one can use the word *humus* to make the idea more palatable) by the lowly earthworm, which is itself part of the food stocks that can be used and transformed by the trees, through the process of photosynthesis, into fiber and, therefore, usable lumber. For example, the balsam fir produces and wears on its bark bubbles or blisters loaded with a resinous pitch so thick and gummy that no insect wants to tackle, and which also protects it from diseases or sudden changes in weather patterns. Balsam fir trees may be attacked in other ways, for example, through their crowns by flying insects that attack firs that are weak or diseased, and this opens holes in the firs' crown pattern that lets the sun in, making it so that grass and berries can now grow. Balsam fir pitch or sap has been used in medicine for a long time. Balsam firs are a variety of conifers that grows abundantly in colder climates and keeps its needle crown even in the winter. The crown retains the heat and permits the tree to start a new growing season sooner when spring comes. The parent varieties of the balsam are white pine, red pine, jack pine, lodgepole pine, a wide variety of spruces. They often grow together in the same stand and interact through their root system with complex web of interlaced underground connections that behaves like a single variety.

Deciduous trees are different in that their limbs are not flexible enough to withstand the weight of snow, and therefore must release their leaves before winter as otherwise, the weight would break most of their branches. Deciduous trees also develop automatic defenses against predators living in their surroundings.

Although it would be pleasant to write a more detailed explanation of how all is connected in nature, I would like to simply make readers aware of what happens when the natural patterns are disturbed. I have been involved in forestry operations for most of my life. What follows is the result of my own observations and study, not the result of intense research, but accurate enough to make the point.

My experience in forestry, specifically in reforestation and harvesting, was mostly acquired in an area of the boreal forest, located for the most part in northern Ontario and part of the Precambrian shield. Next to the rain forests of the Amazon, the boreal forest produces more oxygen and absorb more carbon than any other region in the world. Because of the sheer size of it, it is difficult to give an accurate report of what is being harvested and what is replanted, even for the foresters involved in the process. Each year the government of Ontario publishes statistics on all forestry operations within the province, but these statistics do not reflect the actual operations, and although percentages are given and the whole harvesting operation is called sustainable, the forests products are being harvested at a faster rate than the annual growth can replace the trees even when adding new privately owned plantations. Granted, we are still on the plus side when it comes to carbon absorption and oxygen production, but it is just a matter of time before these proportions change to a negative. In the future we may see a shortage of merchantable timber in the boreal forest. It is true that trees are being replaced, but not to the point of compensating for the ones harvested. It is not my aim to criticize government statistics or start an argument but to present a realistic picture of what happens in nature when it is disturbed by operations such as logging, site preparation, or tree planting.

Clear-Cutting

In the northern countries, conifer greatly outnumber deciduous trees; therefore, the main logging operations are harvesting mostly jack pine, red pine, and white pine, with jack pine being the most abundant at the site of most logging operations. The problem with this variety, mostly used for framing houses is that it cannot be thinned or cut selectively. Because of their proximity to each other the machines must cut all of them or none of them. Even if you leave some of the trees for seed, they do not survive as they depend on each other's roots to withstand wind and storms and are generally down after the first winter. However, leaving a few trees counts as natural regeneration for statistical purposes without the cost and the labor of planting trees. The natural forest, which had formed an integral unit where trees depended on each other and developed protection from bark beetles and airborne insects and regulated the balance between predators and prey, is no longer there. Before the cut, there is usually a great many whitetail and mule deer living in the stand, which provides protection from their natural predators, the wolves, and enough food to sustain the population. Their natural enemies, the wolves, being considered an undesirable species, are generally shot on sight by hunters and farmers, leaving the whitetail and mule deer population almost without a predator except humans. The government of Ontario estimates the population of the whitetail deer to be around four hundred thousand and growing.

After a clear-cut operation, most forms of life in the natural food chain either move out or starve for lack of nutrients. Large animals are no exception. Unless they find another source of food, there will be a reduction of their population. New sources of nutrients are easy to find in previously clear-cut areas where grassy, non-wood species and berries can grow because the land is now exposed to the sun. Grazers, usually large animals, will again multiply until they exhaust their food supply and are forced again to either relocate or starve. The bears and deer have found new sources of food by moving into cities and villages, and like their predecessor the raccoon, they have migrated in large enough numbers to be considered pests. When bears are found in such areas, they are usually drugged and relocated to their natural habitat, but deer are tolerated, protected, and even fed. They can be a nuisance when one is trying to grow a garden, and they are involved in many traffic accidents.

Just a word on what happens when saplings are transplanted to an area other than their natural grounds, where they had developed methods of dealing with bark beetles, budworm, and other pests. Being transplanted is a near-death experience for a sapling, and the use of chemicals known as defoliants is necessary to remove the faster-growing deciduous species such as poplars. Without the defoliants the sapling will not have access to enough sunlight to grow and develop. The use of sprayed chemicals, usually glyphosate, kills the leaves of the faster-growing deciduous trees and permits the coniferous saplings to grow in the sunlight. This also has the effect of killing most parasite insects, and therefore the young trees do not develop protection against these. The budworms, when they move in from another devastated area can enjoy an all-you-can-eat buffet, killing even the healthier trees. In order to preserve valuable timber, more chemicals are sprayed to protect the treetops, which is the source of a good portion of the chemicals causing the degradation of the northern lakes to the point that they are considered a health threat to residents. The rapid growth of commercial lumber operations the use of chemicals and the incredible numbers of wildfire puts the boreal forest in a steady process of decline.

The balance between predators and prey is easily observed in the relation between rabbits and foxes. The rise and decline of each species cover about a three year period from start to completion. The number of foxes increases when rabbits proliferate. The foxes hunt the rabbits and cut down their population to the point where there is a shortage of prey, at which time the cycle starts again. I would enjoy writing more on the delicate balance between species and forested areas, but this could be the topic of a book by itself and is not the subject of *A Wall of Hate*. There is an excellent book dealing with this subject called *The Secret Wisdom of Nature* written by Peter Wohlleben, a German forester. The main point I wish to convey is that all species, including *Homo sapiens*, have this in common: When there is ample food available, they will multiply until they destroy their environment and, with it, their source of food. We humans are now at this point. Using chemicals in the production of food has been a temporary and artificial way of farming, providing abundant cheap food, and humans have responded to it like any other species would: We have proliferated to the point where there will inevitably be a reduction in the number of mouths to feed, either by war, starvation, or natural selection of survival of the fittest, or a combination of all these. Eventually the production of toxic food will stop, falling victim to its own poison. We *Homo sapiens* have no known predators except ourselves.

The main character in Antoine de Saint-Exupéry's book *The Little Prince* lives on a planet so small that if a single baobab were allowed to grow, its roots would invade all the space and consume all the nutrients which would completely destroy the prince's planet. The prince spends some of his time tending to his single flower and his one sheep, but most of his time is spent on uprooting new baobabs. Some seeds, he says, are so evil that they must be uprooted as soon as their shoots stick out lest they destroy the planet.

Disconnected from Nature

I have witnessed a world without the internet; I have witnessed the world without television, without the grid, and without plowed roads in the winter. I remember going to midnight mass on Christmas Eve in a covered sleigh pulled by Nellie, our mare, warmed by preheated bricks and a small woodstove installed by my father, used only for the return trip after the bricks had cooled down. We lived a good six miles (9.6 kilometers) from church, where Nellie would wait patiently for us, covered in her heavy blanket and being fed a portion of oats to help keep her warm. She was in good company with about twenty-five others like her. Returning home was the real treat as Santa Claus had paid us a visit during our absence and we children would find the coveted gift that we had earned by being good for the few preceding days. We then enjoyed a heavy meal and went to bed happy but certainly not hungry.

The farm provided most of what we needed with enough surpluses that were sold to pay for the goods we had to purchase from the general store. We were as close as possible to being self-sufficient, except for gas for the car in the summer, fuel/parts for the tractor, baking supplies, special feed for the cows, and oats for Nellie.

I am not writing this with any kind of twisted desire to lecture younger generations as some folks my age would do, beginning with the traditional and eternal "In my days," but I do want to let my readers know that when I make statements about the advantages of being one with nature, I have personal experience to back them up. A lot has changed since I was a boy, and I cannot help but marvel at what modern technology has accomplished. I appreciate the fact that our youngsters do not have to split wood, round up and milk cows, harness a horse, or clean up the barn. I have adapted, to some degree, to this brave new world that is very different from what I knew as a kid. One thing I must say is that, like most people, I am now closer to my computer and cell phone than I am to nature. I do, however, keep a generator in good working order with enough fuel to last several days, a chain saw, sufficient quantities of nonperishable food to survive for several weeks, and a limited reserve of precious metals that would be negotiable if anything were to happen to our electronic banking system. I am not trying to scare anyone and hopefully conditions will never deteriorate to the point where I have to use these reserves, but sometimes even an ice storm, wind, or flood, or an event indicative of many other new weather patterns, can reduce many areas of the world to survival mode for long periods of time, without any help available for various reasons.

War

Never since the rise of Adolf Hitler has the world been closer to a global war. The United States is hopelessly divided in two with almost zero chance of reconciliation between the two factions, the Left and the Right. The most likely scenario would involve some form of a civil war that would be, to say the least, one-sided in favor of the party that could dispose of the military, the police force, and all the many militia units not registered as part of the armed forces with no lack of eager, well-armed volunteers. President Trump was clear enough in his statement that if the impeachment proceedings against him were to proceed, there would be a civil war in the United States, stating in fact that he had at his disposition all the forces mentioned earlier. Fortunately, this event (Impeachment) is now a thing of the past and proceeded without physical violence. It just gave rise to an incredible amount of chaos.

Canada

Canada, which for a long time has been considered one of the friendliest countries in the world, has recently elected a near majority of members to parliament whose main purpose is to break up of country. These people are taking aggressive actions to separate from the federal government. The United States is divided in two; Canada is divided in four.

Considering the present tensions associated with the economic war going on between Russia, the United States, China, Iran, several countries of the Middle East, and North Korea, it seems that a war of some kind is about to break out, and this could happen as soon as one country feels that it can take the other by surprise and cause enough damage during the first few minutes to paralyze the opponent's nuclear arsenal. Every one of these countries knows that an all-out nuclear war would spell the end of this planet. This may be the only consideration that is holding them back, but all it would take is one small error or an infiltration by terrorists to send these monsters flying. It is very difficult to evaluate how many people would survive, but casualties would be high.

Another likely scenario is that one of these belligerent countries would start with a well-planned attack and proceed to destroy most of the communication satellites on which sophisticated weapons depend for their launching and accuracy. Destroying satellites would not be as devastating as the firing of nuclear weapons but would cause so many other problems that a nation may not survive them. We have become so dependent on the electric grid that the loss of power, even for a few hours, can stop the world in its tracks, leaving us without the tools we consider essential in order to function normally. The modern banking system relies so heavily on satellites, computers, and the power grid that it would not be able to continue operations or even process a single transaction if this technological network were to be severed. We all have been to the bank only to have someone tell us that the computer is down. Fortunately, even if the bank's database has been hacked, we know that at some point operations will resume and everything will return to normal. All our transportation systems rely on the grid and computers. Were this technology to be disrupted, there would eventually be a severe shortage of food and supplies with the inevitable riots and pillaging that would surely leave many dead or severely wounded. Without cell phones, transportation, banking, and the grid, commerce would come to a screeching halt, and especially in large cities, there would be no other option but to stay and fight it out. Escaping to the forest could be an option but not many of our youths have been exposed to nature enough to survive in the wild.

Understanding the Law of Cause and Effect

This additional chapter was added for your information in case you would be interested in becoming one of the advanced workers in the rejuvenation process of our planet. What follows is in no way a teaching program, nor am I trying to set myself up as a guru or teacher. The principles presented here are not official teachings of any group or organization but are simply an outline of actions anyone can take to efficiently start their own personal transformation.

Attempting to make sense of our present situation will require a good deal of understanding of how and why we are on the brink of a major war or ecological catastrophe of some kind. We are now experiencing worldwide the result of the law of cause and effect. The ancients called it karma and had an accurate knowledge of the law itself, its operation, and the inevitable results of setting it in motion. The present chapter may seem unrelated and out of alignment with the title of the book, but it should be evident that if we wish to change conditions and have a considerable influence on events, we must first change ourselves.

Some political figures often make statements that you consider to be pure lies or to be so outrageous that you cannot help from being furious and ready to express your contempt. This is exactly where the author wants you, cranky, mad, and ready to fight. Their aim is to get you contributing to the divisiveness that directs hatred toward an individual or a group so they can then try to transform you into an active member of this wall of hate. Quite simply, if we are to change anything, we first must accept changes to this aspect of our character and liberate ourselves from other people's agendas. This troubled age will require clear thinkers who can remain unaffected by political smut or vicious attacks against our freedom. I do not mean by this that one should ignore what is going on in politics, as everything that has the potential to affect our future is worth examining. You should determine what effect it may have on your life and well-being. The trick here is to remain unmoved and looking for solutions or ways to protect yourself, your family, and your possessions instead of taking sides in the dirty political arena.

The aim is to give you a basic understanding of the nature of the law of cause and effect and will also show how individuals can direct it and work in collaboration with it to improve their condition and find harmony within themselves, with the rest of the world, and with the universe. Even if you feel that you have a good knowledge of the functioning of this law, you could benefit by the reading the explanation presented in this book, keeping in mind that the law of cause and effect is at the base of everything we are experiencing presently, individually and collectively, and it will operate regardless of our belief in it or our denial or misunderstanding of it.

It would be safe to state that nowadays, most people are innately aware that their acts, thoughts, and intentions are causes from which effects are sure to follow, but they are not aware of how this is so or what the results could be. A lot of writers, fortune-tellers, and modern-day motivation gurus talk about karma, quite often without knowing much about it. The word *karma* is used liberally whenever it can be fitted into a diagnosis, presentation, or horoscope, but very seldom is it explained vis-à-vis what it is or how it functions. Perhaps of all the natural laws, karma is the most popular, but it is also the most misrepresented and the least understood, creating much confusion and suffering.

When people are faced with difficulties, most will use the dark humor joke that it must be their karma catching up to them.

They think that they are being punished or disciplined for an act they committed previously, or else they will utter the popular buzz phrase that it must be some form of compensation for an evil act performed in a previous life. How often have you heard someone make the statement when they experience a long period of good health, prosperity, and peace of mind that it must be their karma? They will probably point to some good business decisions they have made or a lifestyle that guarantees them good health. Some, a little less vain, may give credit to others for the help the latter provided, but most always take the final credit themselves.

The workings of the law of Karma are very comprehensible, easy to learn, and can be directed to serve anyone's purposes. The law of cause and effect has the potential to be a great tool in furthering one's advancement on all planes, the material, mental, and spiritual. But we must know what karma is, what kind of actions it responds to, how and when it is activated, and what kind of reactions can be expected from our actions, thoughts, and intentions. This study should leave you with a different view of this great law and inspire you to have confidence in the principles and workings of this and all other natural laws. After you read this and the chapter dealing with personal transformation, you will realize that the new self-help movement, with all that is positive within it, is flawed in many ways with its proponents' explanations of the law of cause and effect. This shortcoming could be the reason why so many people fail to materialize their objectives when using these self-help books and/or after attending expensive seminars. Gurus are in fact directing their customers toward the belief that by using their system, they are making use of some form of little-known divine or cosmic law, which is correct in a way, but then the gurus fail to inform their clients that if one is to solicit the workings of some higher law, one has to come before the court with clean hands and a blank balance sheet. Otherwise it will amount to a waste of time, like praying for peace to a God who resides on a cloud while one continues to project hate or indifference toward humanity, the environment, and all living creatures. Most of the time, what is sought after is material in nature, perhaps even consumer goods, but like Paracelsus stated, "You will transmute nothing until you have transmuted yourself."

(Philipus Aureolus Theophrastus Bombastus Von Hohenhelm 1493-1541, Doctor, chemist, astrologer alchemist who contributed revolutionary practical advances in medicine and is credited with miraculous healings, better known as Paracelsus. He expressed himself with great vigor. This is where the word bombastic came from)

Any attempt to use higher laws in the pursuit of a fortune or worldly goods without observing the cosmic laws of creation is bound to fail. However, these higher laws will serve those who take the time to balance the forces within and who can temporarily function on a higher level of consciousness. The basic idea of modern self-help is that what you have to do to get what you want is to actively want that Cadillac, that house, or whatever until you are blue in the face, work toward attaining your goal by keeping it present at all times in your mind, and make it your principal objective, so much so that it monopolizes your thinking. Granted, this works in a lot of cases, and hard work and tenacity will give results, but one is operating within gross material laws with all the competitiveness and stress that comes with pulling yourself up by your bootstraps. And in any event, this method does not entail the application of higher or cosmic laws.

Karma

The law of karma is not one of resentment, retribution, or retaliation. Karma does not seek to cause equal suffering for any amount of suffering created, and it does not seek to cause rejoicing equal to any joy given by us to others. Its true purpose is to bring to our consciousness a keen realization of the nature of our thoughts, actions, and beliefs. To some, such realization can be brought about only through suffering; to others, karma may make its impression in some other way. But the real object of karma, always, is to make us conscious of our past actions, words, thoughts, and intentions, of their importance to our development toward perfection, and of karma's bearing upon the whole scheme of things. Its greatest effect is in causing us to realize, and teach us a lesson about, the wrongs we have done or to benefit us by the good we have done. Once we have a keen realization of our error, regret it, determine not to repeat it, and do our best to repair the damage we have done, the law of karma is fulfilled and will no longer force its impression on us. And once we have a keen realization of the good that has come from our benevolent acts, the law will cease its operation until once again we perform another good deed. Note that this law does not operate instantly, but its effects will manifest at a time when it will be most meaningful and most likely to teach the lesson to be learned or the benefits to be had in the process of our evolution.

The fear of karma principally exists in the belief that it is of one kind. It is not meant by this that it will always produce the same circumstances or use the same methods in teaching us whatever lesson we need to learn. Most people do, however, think that the purpose of the law or the end that it serves is always to dish out discipline or punishment, and many believe it always manifests as trouble, worry, strife, and physical or mental suffering.

Of course, not everyone believes in the functioning of this law, but even if they do not believe in it, they almost always blame the law for their misfortunes and calamities. Yet still they are not apt to credit karma for the good things that happen to them. Consequently, the word *karma* becomes ominous to many such persons. To them, it always augurs strife and calamity.

Let us not therefore think of karma as some monster against which there is no assurance of safety. Let us consider it in its true light. Karma is not a sort of devious intelligence or genie who keeps you under constant observation, just waiting to pounce upon you with satanic delight and impose severe penalties for faults that you are not even aware of. When fortune fails to come our way and we experience pain and suffering in any way, most of us just ask without thinking the old standard question "What have I done to deserve this?" without really seeking to find out if we have in any way done something that would justify the lesson we are experiencing. But the law will keep working until we have a keen realization of the consequences of our acts, thoughts, or intentions until we make the proper adjustments. The fact is that the law imposes on humans as they react to it, since our conduct, whether good or bad, dictates its operation. Karma, or as we should call it the law of cause and effect, is one of the fundamental cosmic laws of creation. It is impersonal and functions according to its inherent nature. Again, it is neutral in its operation and does not seek to punish or seek revenge on humans in any way. Instead it is simply the logical result of our thoughts, and actions.

To help us in understanding the law, let us visualize a pair of great scales. These scales weigh all our thoughts, words, and actions, whether intentional or unintentional. If you load one tray with hate, cruelty, jealousy, envy, revenge, and other such propensities such as dishonesty, lack of respect for the property of others, lack of concern for the reputation of others, gossip, and hurtful lies that create a disadvantage to someone else, it will create an imbalance that eventually has to be dealt with. When performing these acts like vicious gossip, we may not realize that what we are trying to accomplish is to isolate the target person from a group of his or her friends. There is also the intent to undermine the person's credibility and good name. Although this may be done unintentionally, you can be sure that the opposing tray will be filled with like material that will cause it to eventually balance by making you experience adverse consequences. You can be assured that sometime in the future, you will experience a fateful lesson that will make you realize what results from such conduct. The lessons may be delayed, and sometimes years will pass without any apparent effect, but be assured that someday, the scales will be balanced and you will experience the just workings of the law—and this at the time when it will be the most meaningful to you. I repeat, the law is impersonal in weighing these actions and is not motivated by animosity or malice. As soon as you have realized the reasons for your misfortune, made pledge to discontinue these practices, made an honest effort to make amends, and most of all modified such behavior to guard against erring in such a way again, then the scales may again be balanced. And since the lesson has been learned and the necessary changes made, the law is fulfilled, and no further misfortune will occur until the scales are again set off-balance. Also, if you perform acts of kindness toward others and help others according to the measure of your ability and means, the opposite tray will be filled with like material, and you may experience pleasant occurrences without realizing that your past behavior has merited you the good fortune you are enjoying. In weighing actions, right and wrong, and good and evil, are not even factors as the law is impersonal and will function according to the nature of the contents. Whatever you fill your tray with is your own baggage. The law will function according to the contents you put on the scales, making you experience the same type of elements that you have filled your tray with; hence the famous statement "As you sow, so shall you reap." Of course, this is only a comparison that simplifies the comprehension of the law. Seeing karma as a great pair of scales is something that is easy to visualize and accelerates the understanding of the principles

According to the Emerald Tablet, the spiritual world is ruled by the law of cause and effect "As above, so below." It could be that all our actions, words, and thoughts are registered in some universal memory and become a cause that produces a definite effect in our lives. No one can escape the results of their actions indefinitely. We will eventually attract to ourselves the same type of conditions that we have created regardless of whether we believe in the law or not. But you will ask, "What about the politicians, bankers, CEOs of large corporations, and other businesspeople who have walked away with a good portion of the wealth of the planet and have simply hidden their gold in offshore banks? How come they continue to lead seemingly happy lives, enjoy impunity from prosecution, and even have gained unprecedented power over the common middle-class people who, as a result of these robberies, have been left without jobs and are in many cases homeless?" This is not an easy one to answer, but be assured that in due time, the scales of those people will have to balance.

Each human being, as a free agent, has the power to choose and is being urged by two great and opposing forces. You have the freedom to choose one or the other. Sometimes a person will choose wrongly, while at other times he or she will choose wisely. Therefore, while humankind is a free agent, at the same time each person is a victim of the urges or subject to these urges from within and without. You must have heard this before. It is the foundation for the understanding of the law of karma.

The Law of Karma Is Impersonal

Through ancient teachings and observation, we find that everything that comes into a person's life is the result of his or her own earning and deserving. Consider the example of sticking your finger in an open flame and experiencing the resulting pain and injury. No God or force inflicts the pain upon you. This is not punishment for doing something you should not have done but is the result of natural laws in operation. The pain that comes from such an act is automatic and is not an act of revenge, injustice, or unkindness from God. Nor is it the work of a malevolent being known as the devil. If you stuck your finger in an open flame because you were ignorant of the natural law, then chances are that you learned a valuable lesson and you will not again expose your flesh to open flames or extreme heat. A child who is ignorant of the effects of flame or heat probably learns the lesson like we all learned it, by burning ourselves once or twice. No matter what kind of advice we received by our parents to be careful, we had to find out for ourselves. Ignorance of the law was not even a consideration. Karma is just a method of teaching the great laws and lessons to us without deviation or changes in the result so that we too may learn.

The three tools to use in dealing with karma are quite simple, although they are sometimes difficult to apply:

1. *Realization*

The first point of the law is quite simple: You must realize that your behavior justified a lesson in the first place! For example, directing hateful thoughts toward others could be the first cause of many negative conditions. The law will continue to work negatively until you recognize that you are the cause and until you regret having had hateful thoughts about others.

2. *Correction*

The second point of the law of karma is not so simple. To regain balance, you must adjust the scales. In other words, you must change the behavior. After you have realized the weight and results of your past actions, regretted your actions, and changed your behavior, there is one more step to climb before the scales become balanced.

3. *Compensation*

While it is a giant step to recognize unworthy past actions and make corrections, these two steps by themselves do not clear your conscience of all responsibility. You must show sincerity by trying to the best of your abilities to repair some of the damage you may done to others. While it may not be possible to directly compensate the person or persons whom you have wronged, you can make indirect compensation by practicing charity toward others, keeping in mind that you are offering these good actions in compensation for your previous wrongful actions. This paragraph is very short but to the point. The karmic law is not fulfilled until this step has been taken. Now comes the hard part: forgiving yourself.

There is another aspect of karma that should be considered at this time, and it is collective karma. We carry our share of responsibility for the actions of the groups or societies we belong to or are affiliated with, such as our town or village and our country, and the general actions of humanity in general. It would be wise to perform any positive action we are capable of, not by preaching but by example, to raise the standards of morality and cooperation within our immediate society.

Personal Transformation

The individual is the key to progress in that the advent of a spiritual era must be preceded by the coming of an ever-increasing number of individuals who will understand that the purpose of humanity is to evolve to a higher level.

—Sri Aurobindo

Personal transformation is a long way from the idea, title, and subject of *A Wall of Hate*. This chapter is not a course in human relations or personal improvement, but it does contain suggestions regarding what we can do as individuals to change our outer and inner personality and be a chipper at the wall of hate and not contributors. We have gotten ourselves into environmental problems and situations that are threatening our very survival and that of all species because of the way we think globally and individually, which has caused us to make wrong choices, adversely affecting the planet we live on. The path we are now travelling on is not irreversible, if enough people start to think differently and start to treat our planet as a living thing, then others are bound to follow, and together we may be able to effectively nurse our planet back to some form of health. Granted, this is a long shot, but it is one of the few remaining options still available to us at this point. This one is worth repeating: If we are to change anything, we first need to transform ourselves.

Earth is not only the planet on which we live, but also it serves as a vehicle for the collective soul of humanity. It should be thought of as a living entity and treated as such. While it is true that a great number of us have become aware of what is happening and are making every effort to remedy the situation, it is also true that these efforts are met with fierce opposition from individual and collective self-interests. Not wanting to sound alarmist, I nevertheless think it is evident that if we do not take the necessary steps to safeguard our environment, then humanity in the future, perhaps the not too distant future, will vanish, the victim of its own foolish actions. Many will readily agree with this but are not ready to take the steps necessary to leave a cleaner home for future generations, being too focused on their own immediate gains. Simply put, either we change, or we suffer whatever changes are to come. Of course, this statement will be ridiculed by those who are raping our planet's natural resources for their own interests. Denial is one of the most prominent and most powerful characteristics of the wall of hate.

While some may think that I am trying to set myself up as a teacher or guide, this is not so. I sell nothing and will not give expensive seminars leading naive people to believe that after one weekend, they will come out completely transformed. I consider myself a simple student also in great need of help and guidance. Although some of the principles and actions presented in this chapter may be compatible with the teachings and principles of traditional esoteric organizations, they are in no way lessons coming from me or authorized by these organizations. They are simple changes that we can all adopt to assist our planet and humanity in its quest for maturity and lead the ones ready to accept these change to become one of the body of awakening people chipping away at the wall of hate. You may find that some principles and laws are repeated and often stated in different ways. I will not apologize for this as repetition is at the base of accepting something different and making the necessary changes that will produce results. Just remember that controls exerted on us by populists are also based on repetition until fear and greed become a fact— one that we seem to have accepted on a large scale.

Deep modifications in personality and behavior may sound complicated and out of reach for most people, but it is the first step necessary and the most difficult stage of change and purification, both for us as individuals and for the planet. Our habits are so deeply ingrained into our personality that we harm others and ourselves without being aware of our doing so. It should be clear that to change our habits, we must first change not only the way we think but also the way we act and speak. It should be understood by now that one cannot think one way and experience something different in daily life. Our daily living experiences correspond exactly to what our thinking minds are most engaged with. One cannot be depressed; think about poverty and disease; indulge in gossip, criticism, complaining, and controlling the lives of others; and engage in heavy drinking, overeating, or indiscriminate abusive sex practices and at the same time enjoy a life of abundance, free of disease and worry. This basic universal law is so blatant and so simple that we simply do not realize that the way we think affects our whole lives, our happiness, and/or ability to function as useful and productive members of society.

I will not claim that the methods presented here are infallible or say that they are supposed to be based on established divine laws, but I will ask a question whose answer may surprise you. Do you think that if we follow to the letter the methods known to the ancients and visualize something that has the potential to be harmful to others with a desire to control them or to amass a fortune using improper and immoral techniques, that the natural laws will function or cooperate? They will. These laws are impersonal and indiscriminate, and if directed properly, respecting their limiting requirements of levels of consciousness and firm beliefs, they will eventually manifest as reality, good or bad. Certainly, the universe will not favor one of its children over another as the laws are immutable. However, if our thoughts are directed with the intention of being a channel for these universal laws to support and help humanity and our ecosystem, then all the benevolent forces of the universe will be channeled through us as we work toward the good and evolution of humankind. One does not have to pursue material abundance, as it will be granted at the proper time according to merit and ability. The reverse is also true. If a person dedicates his thinking, words, and actions to unworthy causes and purposes, all the malevolent forces of the universe will be channeled through him. This is the nature of free will. Both sides function equally according to one's decision to serve one or the other.

The Emerald Tablet states, "That which is below corresponds to that which is above, and that which is above corresponds to that which is below." Equivalent to the statement "We reap as we sow." These two statements from two different sources try to teach us that the most important factor that determines the quality of our lives is our thinking. Every thought we allow ourselves to think is itself a creation that we must live with. It attracts conditions of the very same nature and, in fact, determines the conditions we will eventually experience in daily life. The state of your body, whether healthy or sick, the state of your relationships, whether turbulent or peaceful, the state of your fortune, whether prosperous or lacking, is the result of, and entirely conditioned by, thoughts, feelings you chose to entertain, and actions you chose to perform in the past. Your future state will reflect the way you choose to think, feel, and act from this point forward. Unless you are ready to take this first step, you can put down *A Wall of Hate* and forget about it as it will be of no use to you.

Thoughts are the real causative force in life, and although there are others, you choose the quality of your life by choosing the nature of the thoughts you allow or direct your mind to dwell upon. You cannot have one kind of thinking and experience another kind of environment! You cannot change your environment without changing your thinking. The reverse is also true: You cannot change your thinking without changing your environment. This is one of the basic keys to life, and it is an idea that is worth repeating: Your life is transformed by the nature of your habitual thoughts, words, beliefs, and actions. Your everyday situations and experiences depend upon the mental food you supply to your subconscious.

Change your thinking and your life will change too. Thoughts are the first and the most important thing in life, and the ability to think and the free will granted to us to do so is at the root of the major problems humanity is experiencing and the cause of most of our individual problems. But free will can also be considered one of the greatest gifts we have received as human beings if we use it properly.

Karma may be considered one of the basic great universal laws, and its importance should be perfectly obvious to you by now. Stating this as fact will draw no arguments from any thinking person. However, there are certain difficulties you must overcome. First, you must become conscious of the nature of your thinking and decide if there is anything in your thinking pattern that should be modified. Our thoughts are so close to us that the process of changing their pattern is one of the most challenging things one may ever do in life. Thinking patterns derive from the moods one entertains and determine the distinguishing characteristics and the outwardly perceived character of a person.

While the foregoing statements would not be considered the greatest secrets in the universe, they do, in fact, describe the first step you must take in the attainment of happiness, contentment, freedom, and prosperity. You must agree that it would be extremely difficult to be happy and prosperous if your thinking is centered on lack, poverty, disease, hatred, envy, jealousy, and selfishness. Health and happiness will not come easily to anyone who is indulging in excess, be it alcohol, drugs, sex, revenge, or dishonesty. Whatever you wish upon others will come back to you, perhaps in a different form, but whatever the case may be, pleasant or unpleasant events are sure to follow in the future according to the thinking pattern you have been indulging in. Whatever we think is the nature of our future experiences. To summarize this idea and to make it easy to remember and to comprehend: "*A thought is a seed.*"

What You Think Is What You Get

Having stated that your thinking pattern is what determines your experiences in life, I ask that now you consider the difficulties in changing a habitual thinking pattern, and I suggest a method that could completely overhaul this pattern without your having to resort to the application of willpower and determination like some methods ask you to do. I am not saying that this will come easily and that all you will have to do is read *A Wall of Hate* and then everything will fall into place, but the method presented here does make it much easier to determine the nature of your predominant thoughts, points out certain things that you may think should be changed, and guide you in reprogramming yourself on all levels, physical, mental, and spiritual, by submitting new material to your subconscious, which has the power to manifest permanent changes in all areas of your life. A new habit must be conceived in such a way that it will replace the old pattern without friction or argument from the ego. Results in most cases are almost immediate. In the section dedicated to karma, you find many useful tips and methods. You cannot erase the past, but you can, by making the necessary changes in your thinking and by correcting your behavior, make the transition more bearable and even enjoyable.

To a certain extent, you will have to make use of the power of your will in order to replace your thinking pattern with a new selection, but after the new pattern emerges and is continued with persistence, the habit is formed and established as your normal and regular way of thinking. Then it will be relatively easy to maintain the new set of rules, especially since you are bound to notice new, positive, and pleasant changes in your personality and to your overall experiences in daily life. It will then become easier and easier to remain steadfast in the new orientation. The new behavior will become part of your personality and will be reflected in your social life, your business life, and other areas of your life.

As we are considering methods that may be new to you, you should be realize that to bring about the desired results, you will have to modify some of your most basic and, sometimes, most cherished beliefs. You are entirely free to reject some, if not all, of what is presented here, but if you would consider these laws or options and decide to accept them, even temporarily, soon a new horizon and life pattern will open for you. Most of these are very ancient and have been stated by the philosophers and prophets of every age, but most of the time they were enrobed in texts or expressed in undecipherable symbols that are not user-friendly and are difficult to understand for the noninitiated. Or they were simply veiled in allegories or parables. This certainly was the case for the ancient alchemists who, far from revealing their principles and secrets, enveloped them in symbols and texts that could only be understood by those properly trained, so that no one but the properly initiated and very patient would know their true meaning. If, after working with these new beliefs for some time, you feel more comfortable with your original options, then you are entirely free to go back to them. But these new beliefs are worth considering, especially if you hope to become one of the chippers at the wall of hate.

Here are some of the beliefs that you could adopt temporarily to test them out. Remember that it is not necessary that you believe in a law for it to operate. If a natural law operates in a certain way, then it will keep operating in such a manner regardless of whether you believe in it or not.

These principles or laws are considered part of the basic set of laws governing the universe and are therefore immutable. They are submitted for your consideration as follows:

- The universe is one.
- Humankind is dual in nature.
- There is a universal consciousness that permeates the universe.

- We are here to assimilate lessons and to refine the personality of our souls.
- We are submitted to reincarnation until we achieve full reintegration with the source. (Optional)
- There are universal and immutable laws governing the universe.
- Karma is the law of cause and effect.
- There is no good or evil except for that which humanity creates.
- Each human being is a free agent, free to choose between good or evil in his or her thoughts, words, and actions.
- The first and most dangerous dragon that one faces is the ego.
- Consciousness is the greatest force in the universe.
- This one is worth repeating: Consciousness is the greatest and most creative force in the universe when properly directed.
- The creative forces of the universe are present within us.
- The power to transform or transmute is within, not without.
- That which is cosmic is infinite and eternal.

Some of these are not easily accepted by the finite human mind, but in the event you do decide to temporarily accept these few principles as being sound and true, I now ask you to consider methods by which your character defects, addictions, and unwanted habits can be transformed in the fastest and most painless way possible.

First, we should consider a few principles of addiction, the nature of addiction, and the way to effectuate positive and permanent changes. It is not my intention here to criticize the many organizations such as AA as they accomplish a lot of positive work. There is, however, the disturbing fact that most, if not all, members are required to admit publicly that they have an addiction and are powerless in their struggle against alcohol, drugs, sex, or some other obsession. They are then instructed to submit their problem to a force greater than themselves, which is little understood, different, and apart from themselves. In other words, this is like going to a counter and telling the clerk, "I have this addiction; fix this for me, please." While it is not my intention here to discourage anyone from believing in a God outside themselves, I do intend to say that seeking an external deity detracts from the fact that the patient's problem is internal and not external and that the forces capable of changing the patterns are not external but within the person's consciousness. Although this may sound like a bold statement, it is in every way in accord with cosmic laws.

One of the great masters used one phrase that seems to be a mystery to us, but that should not be so. When he said, "I am the resurrection and the life," he was referring not to his outer self, his body or earthly personality, but to the divine spark within him that could accomplish the miracles with which he is credited. He also said, "The Father and I are one." This has led the Christian church to adopt the belief that the Master is the only incarnation of the great heavenly Father, who is located somewhere in the sky and inaccessible to us mere humans, unless we go through the intricate liturgies of a church service in order to access the wisdom of the Master to some degree. The Master also said, "What I have accomplished, you can also, and even greater." This statement is more in line with the ancient texts that teach that humankind is dual in nature. A human is a divine being having an earthly experience to master the elements of his or her personality by trials and tribulations and to serve the creative forces of the universe by helping others in their evolution. Every mystic knows that to attain some degree of mastership over destructive forces, one must look inside, search for the divine element present there, as it is in every human being, and direct it properly to modify external conditions. There is in each one of us a part of the divine force that created the universe, and every human being has the power to direct that force. Without realizing that we are doing it, we are doing this all the time—yes, in ways both good or bad.

Getting back to addictions, when an addict shows up at a group meeting, the two most powerful words in any language are used against the recovering addict. This could very well be the reason it is believed that an addiction is incurable and that once the pattern is established, one will have to fight it for the rest of one's life. What then are these magical words? These words are simply "I am." These words can be tremendous assets if used as a decree for self-improvement, but they work equally well positively or negatively. When you say the words "I am," you are making a statement that what you are decreeing is in fact what you are, and this sends the message to the higher consciousness within you that this is the way things are, or are going to be and will class it as such and if your outer-self accepts the statement as true, your subconscious will classify it and make it a law. The statement "I am" is neither positive or negative and can be used both ways.

Suppose you were to make a statement such as "I am an alcoholic." After making this statement, can you imagine being anything but an alcoholic? The same is true with the statement "I am powerless." Guess what? You've created your reality, and you truly accept the idea that you can do nothing but accept these facts, even though you are the one who got yourself into this mess.

Whenever you use "I am not" statements, you are also directing the events or conditions you will experience in the future, as your experiences will unfold according to your beliefs. Every time you use "I am not," you cut yourself off from any higher form of help from your divine nature. There is also a very negative side to "I am" statements like: "I am sad," "I am sick," "I am lonely," "I am poor," etc. With these being your accepted beliefs, you certainly can perceive how they affect you and limit your thinking, actions, and freedom to choose.

Before we proceed further with this "I am" thing, it would be well to open a new subject, specifically, a question that nearly everyone is seeking an answer to or an explanation of: "Who am I?"

There is an ontological statement that says, "God created man in his image. He breathed into his nostrils the breath of life, and man became a living soul." The soul is incorruptible. It is everywhere—within every cell and atom of the body—and is an integral part of the universal force that created the universe. Perhaps you are beginning to perceive that the soul is part of what we usually refer to as God; the creative faculties reside within us and can be directed to accomplish what some may consider miracles.

Besides the body and the soul, there is another element we can call the personality, and this is the part that must evolve and eventually attain spiritual perfection. Each human being is born a free agent and has the power to make decisions, even ones that are detrimental to one's own health, prosperity, happiness, peace, and well-being of that of other persons. This subject could itself be the whole topic of a book; the present text is only an attempt to make you aware that life is within you and that the most creative forces of the universe are within you. This life force within you will not question your beliefs, but because you have been given the privilege of being a free agent, it will accept them as true and bring into your life those experiences that are in accord with those beliefs. This is an oversimplification, but if you accept the idea that you can change your life by changing your beliefs, then you are on the right track. The fact that should be remembered is that humankind is dual but is composed of three different elements, soul, spirit (personality), and body. You have probably heard this great truth referred to as the Father, the Son, and the Holy Ghost. So, whenever you use these words "I am," be aware that you are using the most potent force in the universe, which is within and which has the power to bring into your life the reality and experiences that are compatible with your accepted beliefs.

A word of caution is in order. It is obvious that the preceding chapter deals with the use of affirmations or decrees. When you decree something that is entirely contrary to your beliefs, it cannot be transmitted to your inner self as a true statement or as your true belief. The power of affirmation is real and cannot be denied, but there is also a dangerous side to this. For example, if you were to make an affirmation such as "I am rich," it will not work and will not bring into your life the wealth you want if you cannot imagine the final result and do not truly believe that it is already done, an accomplished fact. Your inner and outer selves both know that proclaiming the statement that you are rich is an untruth, especially if you are struggling with two jobs and earning minimum wage. You, however, can make statements that will be accepted by both sides without any opposition, will get everything working for you, and in the process will change and improve your personality. Instead of stating an untruth such as "I am rich," use something that will get seen and unseen forces working on your behalf. Simply affirm, "I am the life and the power of my financial freedom," and when you make the statement, first be aware that you are talking to all elements of yourself, especially the fragment of divinity that is within you, and next consider it a seed that will eventually germinate and grow. Such is the law of attraction.

Of course, what is presented by motivators is true. You have to be clear on what you want, but what is presented here will put you in a position where you will monitor your statements, thoughts, and actions, knowing that the seed you plant is positive, will germinate and become what you have decreed. This sounds like gardening, but consider the fact that when you place a seed in the ground, you do not question the fact that it will eventually sprout and produce results in due time, even though you may not be able to see the results immediately. In other words, you accept the results as true and possible without seeing them. Practice patience and do the best you can in working toward your goals without stress, and the stated decree will manifest.

An affirmation such as "I am an alcoholic" can have devastating effects. A statement such as "I am powerless" also has a devastating effect. Suppose that instead you were directed or encouraged to use affirmations of a different kind, shifting the weight of your problem directly onto and into yourself without any external intervention of any kind and by which practice you were to become empowered, hopeful, and efficient. You're right, it could be stated as "I am" affirmation, but in a different context altogether. Just consider the difference it would make if you were to state clearly and confidently, "I am now free from the power of alcohol. I am now sober. I am the life and power of my freedom."

Habits, Addictions, and Obsessions

Who you are is limited by what you think you are.

A habit, according to the Oxford dictionary, is a "regularly repeated behavior pattern; a pattern of behavior that is repeated so often that it becomes typical of one's personality, although the person is unaware of it."

Solidly established habits are extremely difficult to modify. The formed habit liberates one from the task of reasoning every time it would be called for. One does not have to use willpower to drive a car. By habit, we enter the vehicle, oftentimes without thinking about it, turn the key, and drive away without having to debate the pros and cons. Accelerating, braking, and all the other actions that are quite complex are performed without effort on the part of the driver and are an automatic response. The same goes for many of the daily actions we perform, such as brushing our teeth, shaving, bathing, and cooking. Remember the first time you drove a car? It probably required all your attention and concentration to steer the vehicle around the parking lot, until you became familiar with the set of actions required to operate the car safely.

Generally, the forming of a habit is the result of repetition. A habit changes something perceived as difficult into something that can be easily performed. This is the good or positive side of habit forming, but there are many differences between habits and addictions.

An addiction, while it could be called a habit, is different. It could be defined as an obsession with certain emotional or physical sensations one may experience when indulging in the absorption of certain substances or in emotional states that the mind knows is harmful but cannot resist without great effort. Things that could be classified as obsessions include depression, anger, jealousy, vanity, meanness, hypocrisy, selfishness, dishonesty, laziness, hatred, fear, and, in another category of course, substances such as alcohol, drugs, and other temporary mood- or mind-altering things. One of the pioneers of modern psychiatry, Dr. Carl Jung, pinpointed most of these as hurtful propensities and things that one would have to change in order to achieve and maintain health, happiness, and prosperity.

Surprisingly, it can be relatively easy to install a new set of thoughts that will lead to habitually proper actions and attitudes. The "I am" decree, if stated clearly and positively, will convey the message to your inner self that you are serious about changing conditions and will accept this as true and as something you wish to experience in your life.

The Ancient Alchemists

Although many unscrupulous individuals claimed to have the knowledge and ability to fabricate gold from base metals, the alchemists of ancient times should be differentiated from the so-called puffers who defrauded many greedy and gullible investors out of their life savings. Whether some succeeded in the transmutation of lead into gold or not is not a concern of traditional alchemy as practiced by the Rosicrucians today. By virtue of their philosophy, they are practicing spiritual alchemy, striving to improve themselves on the human plane.

Nothing makes it possible to affirm in all certainty that gold can be produced alchemically.

The traditional Alchemy Guild adepts are effectively working in labs and experimenting with metals, but the first step whether working with spiritual alchemy or with metals is the same in that the personality of the operator is to be transmuted first if such a person seeks to become a channel for constructive universal forces. This first step, called calcination, is the act of replacing every defect with its opposite. This can be liberating and can also be the starting point of an incredible journey toward the reintegration of the operator with the First Cause. It is in this spirit that the following exercise is presented here.

What You Think Is What Grows

Whatever you allow to occupy your mind will magnify in your life. Whatever the subject of your thoughts may be, good or bad, the law you set in motion works, and the condition grows. Any subject that you keep out of your mind tends to diminish in your life. Whatever you do not use atrophies. The more you think of grievances, the more trials you will continue to experience. The more you think of the good fortune you have had and the future plusses to come, the more good fortune will come to you.

The previous statement could draw some arguments, but overall, almost everyone will agree that it is a sound principle. The problem is in implementing it into our daily lives. As you will see, everything that is presented here is easily applicable. One needs only to follow a few rules, keeping in mind that thoughts do determine the nature and quality of our experiences.

First and foremost, determine the items that should be changed in your life. By this, I mean all habits and undesirable traits of character that you would like to remove from your personality. If you are honest about this, you will not find this step to be an easy one, even if you use the tools presented here.

Second, replace the undesirable behavior or habit with its opposite. This one is also worth repeating. Suppose you have an addiction of some kind and try to rid yourself of it. If you concentrate on the affliction itself, it will only be reinforced and will surely be harder to eliminate because it has become the object of your creative thinking. The ego will not easily relinquish the power it has over you; it will require constant application of willpower just to keep it in check. In other words, and for purposes of clarity, concentrating on the opposite virtue and repeating it will brainwash you into accepting the new ideas as your new values.

Third, install the new opposite file into your brain and permanently delete the unwanted item. Repetition and the belief that the new qualities are now part of your personality will install them and eventually make them your new standards.

Following is a table to help you determine the nature of some of the things in your life that you may wish to change. Feel free to add or delete any item you feel does not apply to you and to add new things you would like to erase from your mind. You should not concentrate on the fault to be eliminated as this will bring it forward as the main object of your thinking and will manifest as strife and opposition if you try to change it because it is already an accepted belief. Work on its opposite condition, which will eventually become part of your new accepted beliefs and manifest for you most positively. Here are some examples:

Negative	Positive
Anger	I am patient.
Jealousy	I am trusting.
Resentment	I am friendly.

Pride	I am humble.
Vanity	I am humble.
Deceit	I am frank.
Hypocrisy	I am sincere.
Laziness	I am diligent.
Aggressiveness	I am considerate.
Fear	I am courageous.
Superstition	I am rational.
Lack of will	I have willpower.
Food	I am healthy.
Drugs	I am free.
Alcohol	I am sober.
Sex	I am in control of myself.
Emotional problem	I am rational.
Your choice	I am "......" I am
Hatred	I am love.

The last two items deserve serious consideration as they are the base and the two phases of the power on which the universe is built. One is constructive and the other is destructive, but both are necessary and complementary in the creation of matter and the evolution of consciousness. Pardon me for the ugly analogy, but in one sense they may be compared to the two poles of a battery, positive and negative. One pole alone could not produce power or energy to perform any work and would therefore be useless. What happens when a battery goes dead? One pole, the positive, expended all the energy it had accumulated, which was absorbed by the negative, transforming both poles into neutral units, each unable to produce results without the presence of the other. The poles are balanced but cannot produce any useful work for lack of complementary and opposite energy. The expression "to recharge your batteries" is appropriate here, but positive current is necessary for this to happen.

Let's Make Peace with Love

The word *love* is one of the most used in any language but also one of the most misunderstood. If you look in a dictionary, you will find a definition that describes love as "wanting the good of another beside oneself." This is an accepted description, and love is viewed for the most part as an emotional experience or state of mind. This is, however, a pale definition compared to what love is in the absolute. Among the qualities associated with the human soul, love is its most powerful attribute in the service of good, provided that such love has been awakened and put into practice.

Most people are capable of loving, but only in a very limited way. Many people feel love and direct it toward members of family, groups or individuals for whom they have an affinity, and perhaps even all of humanity, though it is not possible to love all humans equally, as we have not yet reached this degree of spiritual evolution. While it may not be possible to love everyone equally, it is mandatory that we hate no one—and in this fast-paced world where hate seems to be the dominant force, this is not an easy task. Neutrality may be the key, and even if one must defend one's own or one's family's interests, it can be done without the hate factor. We do not have to like or even approve of someone else's actions, but after ensuring that a person causing us harm has been neutralized, we should consider the experience as part of the learning process. The offending person is left to activate his/her own karma so that they too may learn. While this may not be the ideal solution, it is better to be neutral than to hate. One can concentrate on and take positive actions to improve one's health, peace of mind, and prosperity without the paralyzing effects and the karmic reactions of hate.

Universal Love

Much has been said and written about universal love, but it is difficult to express and convey to another something that has not been experienced. If we are to change and evolve, we must love ourselves first by accepting our own imperfections and then express this universal love without the egocentric or selfish attitude so often perceived as the key to being strong and confident. Your realities in life are the direct results of what you project into the world. Love or hate will come back to you and determine your own perception of the world. And remember that we have been given total power and free will to express either love or hate in our personal lives.

As can be seen, these are opposites that cannot be present at the same time. One cannot express love and hate at the same time. One cannot be honest and dishonest at the same time. One cannot be drunk and sober at the same time.

Periods of meditation to evaluate these changes and to make a final decision as to which habits you would like to add or modify will be necessary, but it is well worth the effort.

Love in the Absolute

Although we consider it a mere mental state, love is much more than that in the universal cosmic reality. It is a force, even the primary force that underlies all creation and is responsible for the attraction of nonmaterial particles of light of different polarities that form atoms, which in turn are attracted to other atoms to form molecules, which are the building blocks of what we perceive as matter. This is a very simplistic explanation used only to make you realize that the universe is composed of particles of light united by the power of attraction or love.

There are now an incredible number of gurus attracting much attention by selling seminar tickets, videos, or books with titles that usually contain the phrase *universal laws* or *law of attraction*. While these gurus may be right on many points, this law defined and presented as complex and difficult to understand is the universal and immutable law of love, that of two polarities uniting by the power of attraction to manifest creation. We can easily comprehend this law of duality and creation by referring to ourselves as being dual in polarity with male and female uniting in love to create offspring. We can also easily agree that atoms of hydrogen and oxygen attract each other to form the most abundant substance in the universe: water. While the process cannot be observed in a material sense, we are conscious of its effects and accept the principle of duality and polarities without arguments.

This law of attraction is present everywhere in the universe and perhaps beyond and is ever reacting to our cocreator's power in shaping the life we experience. Infinity, timelessness, and supreme power are not principles that are easy for the finite human brain to comprehend, but if we are to use them effectively, we first have to accept them and make use of the laws and tools that were given to us as a birthright. The choice is yours. If you want to be healthy, you should love health. If you want prosperity, you should love prosperity, and then it shall be given unto you without the hassle of greed and dishonesty. If you want love, you first must project love. This is not meant to be an essay about the nature of God or of the universe, as it is best to leave those teachings to the ancient traditional esoteric organizations. The only thing I would like readers to remember is that you cannot express hate and love at the same time, but you are free to choose the nature of your thinking at any time. Love creates. Hate destroys.

Setting goals at the conscious level limits you to a very low chance of potential effectiveness in achieving these goals or making changes. The struggle comes from the fact that you have been working against the immense power of your subconscious mind. When you visualize the fulfillment of a desire that is in perfect harmony with the good, the whole universe collaborates and assists in its materialization. When properly concentrated upon, your "I am" becomes a thought form that eventually manifests in your physical world.

Let us consider one of the great laws of creation of the universe: The visible emanates from the invisible, and the finite proceeds from the infinite. The same is true of changes you wish to make in your life and/or personality. First, decide what change you want to make, then visualize yourself, speaking, and behaving accordingly. Next comes the difficult part: Just release the old habit or thought with confidence that universal law is taking care of the matter and that what you seek in its place will manifest according to the laws of justice and love and depending on where and when it will have the most positive impact on your life. When visualizing the outcome, you should be aware that the subconscious reacts more to your true feelings and emotions than to actual words. Mix some emotions with your request by seeing what you seek as clearly as possible and feeling the joy of already having it. You probably have heard that some people are so developed that they can produce instant materialization, but for the rest of us, there is a time element involved.

Cogito Ergo Sum

"I think, therefore I am" is a conclusion René Descartes came to. No one would argue that we humans, in our daily lives, have the capacity and ability to make choices about most of the situations we encounter daily. We even have the responsibility to do so. What is not so obvious to us is that we can also use this freedom of choice to shape events that have not yet occurred. We have been given the capacity to anticipate the future and to shape it according to the way we want to shape it, using the tools of thought, memory, and imagination.

The development of this aspect of free will marks a giant step in the evolution and development of the individual. By using free will this way, you can be certain that you are taking the future of your life into your own hands and that the results will influence and even determine you station in life. Having determined that we can make choices in the present as well as in the future, you should remember that free will is neither total nor absolute. Sometimes our choices are necessarily limited by our environment, such as our family circle, our social and cultural framework, our religious context and dogma, the laws of the country we live in, and natural events. These conditions originate from sources outside ourselves, and we are often limited by these external conditions and events that we did not cause and that did not originate in our thought process, but it should be remembered that where we are now is the result of our previous actions, words, beliefs, and thoughts. If you accept adversity for what it is, a tool and perhaps a test in the process of evolution, then you do not have to be passive about adversity and accept it. Instead, you can see it as a great help and recognize that you have the power to change conditions. The first thing is to sincerely ask how you can change your negative conditions and then remain open to any suggestions.

Negative Thinking

Let's define what is meant by negative thoughts: any thought of failure, disappointment, or trouble; any thought of criticism, spite, jealousy, or condemnation of others, or of self-condemnation; and any thought of sickness, accidents, or limitation. A dependable guide is that any thought that is not constructive should not be permitted to dwell in your mind as it will eventually cause havoc. A negative problem can be examined from another perspective. Examine the problem objectively, and if you do not know the solution, ask your subconscious for the best possible solution. Forget about the problem, and rest assured that a solution will come to you in due time, but do not give directions as to what should be done or by what method the problem is to be resolved. The results will surely surprise you. And after a certain amount of time and practice, a pattern will be established whereby you dwell not on problems but on solutions. Just about every self-help author has stated this in a different way. Just remember that the thoughts that will shape your future are the ones you allow your mind to dwell upon. Negative thoughts have no power when properly dealt with. Even when you are watching or reading news that could be depressing or revolting, ask yourself what you can do about the situation, but do not get emotional about a situation you can do nothing about as this will only harm you and will deprive you of the energy that should be used for performing more constructive actions and dealing with other situations. This is not easy to do when you see or read of the atrocities committed by some terrorist groups or about the sometimes disgusting actions of governments, large corporations, and other organizations, but instead of getting outraged, just send thoughts of love and healing toward the victims of those situations. This will accomplish more than any hateful thought you could direct toward the predators. This also has the value of attuning you with the creative forces of the universe.

Mental Creation

We should know and be aware of the value and danger of mentally creating and the goodness and the evil that lies in the power to mentally create. We know that if we hold in our minds a picture and give it the vibrations of a living possibility, and if we proclaim that it is or will be, then we bring it about. We create it in the world of the absolute which transfers our creation to the world of reality, the material manifestation. We know that the things that we have created in our imagination and that we have allowed to pass to a higher level of consciousness are likely to be crystallized into material form. We must therefore be pure-minded. We must keep the chamber of mental alchemy clear and set it to such high standards that no evil thought, no evil admission, and no unholy concept is allowed to invade our mind, where the mental creation may grow and eventually be born in the world of our own reality.

Caution is the keyword regarding the process of mental creation, and one should take heed of these facts when directing universal laws in the acquisition of worldly goods.

A Wall of Hate is not meant to be used as a self-help course, but I must present certain facts and make the reader aware of some of the dangers involved before anyone attempts to use these suggestions.

Unless you can accept that the forces capable of transforming matter and conditions are within you and not somewhere in the sky, any attempts you make to change conditions from without will bring frustration and, in many cases, failure.

If you truly believe that your request has already been granted, your present conditions may give you evidence to the contrary, but you have to be assured that what you have created already exists as a fact in the universe and that it will show up in your life when the time is proper.

The divine part of you, responsible for your breathing, healing of wounds, digesting of foods, and all that we call the involuntary functions, is programmable and, in fact, is continuously being programmed by your thinking. It will always bring into your life that which is in accordance to your true beliefs.

Requests for anything that will cause harm to others or requests that are motivated by ego and vanity do not stand a chance and will produce negative karma.

Any hateful thought or wish for revenge will not affect the target but will turn against the operator and, in due time, will produce the same kind of conditions of hate and strife. It may also manifest as sickness or poverty.

Always address these divine laws with the most reverend attitude and a clean mind, and know that whatever your request, it must include benefits for others as well as for you.

This most important point is worth repeating: Have faith that after you make an "I am" decree and have stated, "It is accomplished," what you seek already exists on the higher plane, which means that you have met with success.

Not believing that it is already done and paying too much attention to present conditions equals failure.

Remember that when you are visualizing, what you are feeling is one of the most important factors in determining success or failure. You must experience in your imagination the same feeling you would have if you were living the experience. This feeling is of the physical body and is the necessary counterpart to manifesting the desired condition on the material plane.

Once you have started to get tangible results, be careful and *never* let your imagination wander or dwell on something you do not want to materialize in your life. Like the old saying goes: Be careful of what you wish for as it may manifest in your life.

The Law of Assumption

Again, assume that what you visualize is already an accomplished fact in the cosmos and that it will manifest in your material world when it is best for you. Before making a request, always go through a session of self-examination and offer to do whatever may be necessary to correct and balance your karmic condition. After assuming that what you have requested is already an accomplished fact and that you are just waiting for its manifestation, you must make sure you do not begin to live in a dream state that would lead you to neglect your present duties or the actions that you should be taking.

What Happens at Birth

It would be well at this time to consider what ancient texts and ancient teachings have to say about the birth and life of a human being. This will help you better comprehend the material presented in this chapter.

Each human being is born essentially without a choice. At the time of birth, the infant ceases to operate as a parasitic form of life and begins to operate as an independent life-form. At the moment the infant inhales its first breath, two different and opposite principles, soul and material body, unite, and this union forms a third condition, namely, a psychic body that will remain in constant contact throughout the person's life with both the universal soul that now resides within the infant and the material body with its five senses. This body regulates heartbeat, blood flow, the growing of fingernails, and all the involuntary functions whose operations we have so much trouble understanding. In addition to the two principles, body and universal soul, united in this new body, the newborn is endowed with a unique personality for which it is responsible to develop spiritually, morally, and materially. Humankind has free will, and this psychic body will accept anything the outer person truly believes to be truth and will transmit it to the part of soul that has the power to materialize. The forces that can transform an idea into a materialized reality reside within this body and will proceed without argument and with complete accuracy in directing the manifestation. Although this explanation is not very scientific and is by no means complete, it will help the reader to understand what is meant by the statement "Thoughts are things."

Visualization

I hope that by now you have a clear understanding of the process of visualization and what material should be concentrated on when you are requesting assistance from the cosmic. The following is a true story and is used to demonstrate the obvious mistake most people make when seeking assistance. Its other purpose is to make you aware of how to direct requests in a way that will not guarantee results but will greatly increase and most likely determine the chances of manifesting in the physical world that which you are seeking.

A woman with three kids, divorced from a husband who paid only the absolute minimum for the support of their children, was working a lousy job that did not pay enough for her to afford decent housing or transportation. In desperation, she sought help from metaphysical principles.

She concentrated on getting a new job. Indeed, the only thing she could think of that would be a solution to her problems was to get a new and better job. When asked why she wanted a new job, she said it was to provide adequately for her three children, move into a better house close to schools, and buy a car she could use to drive the kids to school in. As can be seen, getting a new job was not her real priority. Moving to a better location, buying a car, and having the funds to provide a good life for her family were the real issues.

She easily came to an understanding that these things were exactly what she wanted and decided to visualize her family living in a good house with her having the use of a good vehicle and providing adequately for her kids—and even having a surplus for emergencies. She realized that she had limited the way in which these things should come to her by limiting the creative forces with her specific request of a better job.

The woman started concentrating on her real wishes. Interestingly, a few months later, she was offered new employment she had never considered before. Being a university graduate, she found that the position fit with her qualifications perfectly with a salary more than double of what she'd been paid at her old job.

It could be argued that this could have happened anyway, even if she had not concentrated on her wishes, and such may be the case, but remember that visualizing the life you wish to live in the future without imposing conditions on the cosmic is powerful stuff. The first element here is called faith, and the faith I'm speaking of is quite different from what religion teaches us.

The Price of Freedom

Freedom has a price. In order to function as a freer individual, you must be in control of all your emotions, even the most difficult ones. This requires courage and goes contrary to a natural tendency present in most of us to judge rapidly and to get emotionally involved even if we can do nothing about a situation. Manipulators and advertisers are aware of this. Getting us emotionally involved is one of the most powerful tools they have at their disposal to exert control over us. Control of our emotions by others is so subtle that at times it is not recognizable for what it really is. Every vitriolic or absurd statement made by our leaders is probably well planned, and the results are so effective that, by our getting upset about it, we lose control over our logical thinking process and, in fact, contribute to the divisive power of the wall of hate.

Everything in our modern society is intended to exert control over our emotions. It is very tempting to mentally retaliate against some of these leaders who make absurd statements or take terrible actions, even wishing them ill, but the moment we do this, we lose control over our own intellectual process and contribute to the divisive influence that keeps them in power.

Afterword

We cannot or should not count on our government or on corporations to implement changes that would be beneficial to the environment or that would give the working people and the middle class more freedom or power. In a world of hierarchy, those on top need those at the bottom to stay at the bottom. If the masses were to wake up to their power as creators and reclaim their abundance through use of their inner mental powers and an understanding of how the universe works, the present hierarchy would not be sustainable.

The early part of the previous century, especially the 1920s, was a time of celebration, joy, and prosperity. People were starting to realize that the new technology could provide them with a kind of freedom never-before experienced by humans. It was a time of new thought, happiness, and abundance. There is no telling where we would be now if this had not been interrupted, but interrupted it was.

What they called the Great Depression had profound and long-lasting effects, especially on the workers, who after that era developed a sense of mistrust, fear, and hatred, which they passed on to following generations and which is still very alive today. The Depression was not only an economic one. It was also a time of great personal depression. People are not generally friendly, happy, or creative when fighting for survival. They are also not very open to new ideas that could help them regain their freedom. A hungry person will think mostly of food. A homeless person will think mostly of shelter. It is not the time to talk to those people about the law of attraction or of the study of natural and higher laws that could be of help to them. They will likely continue with their depressed state and attract to themselves the very conditions they fear. Yes, the Great Depression was a blow from which the masses never recovered. The same cycle is still with us and is very active, engendering the same kinds of fears, of lack and scarcity, and keeping the masses in a quasi-permanent state of depression. The name has changed, though. These periods are now called recessions, but the results are the same. We are programmed into a state of constant depression by the media. And especially with the new phenomenon of openly authoritarian politicians supported by an incredible number of eager and aggressive followers totally dedicated to the elimination of personal freedom for anyone different, it is enough to instill a feeling of insecurity, helplessness, and depression. No one feels safe anymore, except perhaps those who proclaim that war, guns, and domination amount to the only possible solution to our present problems.

Those who overcome this vicious cycle and start programming their own future, regardless of their present conditions, will be the pioneers of the coming new age. The task of rebuilding a society based on sound moral principles will rest on the shoulders of these few who dare believe in themselves, trust the laws of the universe, and use them to benefit themselves and humankind.

Please forgive me if you think *A Wall of Hate* could be perceived as a recruiting commercial for esoteric organizations. Although ideally more people would adhere to the principles espoused by such organizations, do not forget that no religion, group, or organization has a monopoly on wisdom and knowledge. You do not have to join any group, sect, or order to be morally strong and be of service to society. However, the traditional groups have the advantage of being able to put you in contact with others who are like you, walking question marks who are seeking the meaning of life and creation. Also, these organizations provide instructions that are meant to develop one's higher faculties, this without seeking to polarize members or brainwash them into believing anything that is being taught. One is always free to hold beliefs that are different. However, there comes a time when one, after proving the soundness of the teachings, freely adopts the principles as a way of life—and this is where the real personal transformation begins. The organizations and fraternities mentioned or alluded to in *A Wall of Hate* have stood the test of time and are linked to traditional roots and to the wisdom of the ancients.

Dear reader, brother or sister, I wish upon you, peace, happiness, perfect health, prosperity, and personal power. By working together as freethinkers toward a better system, we will find that the present crisis does not have to be

THE END.

Bibliography

Edward Barneys, *Propaganda* 1928.

Dyer, Wayne W. *Change Your Thoughts—Change Your Life.* Carlsbad: Hay House, 2008.

Gore, Al. *An Inconvenient Truth.* 2008.

Lewis, H. Spencer. *Rosicrucian Principles for Home and Business.* Supreme Grand Lodge of A.M.O.R.C., October 1929

Wattles, Wallace D. *The Science of Getting Rich.* 1910.

Wohlleben, Peter. *The Secret Wisdom of Nature.* New York: Random House, 2017.

Printed in the United States
By Bookmasters